"This is a significant book on a topic that cc
tant. What we believe about the nature of
not risk having an underdeveloped or sub-biblical a....
such a central Christian concern. To put it as plainly as possible: I
want every one of our students to read this book and to reflect deeply
on its teachings, since what Dolezal seeks to explain is nothing less
than the historic doctrine of the Christian church."

— Jonathan L. Master, Professor of Theology and
Dean of the School of Divinity, Cairn University

"The road to doctrinal decline is not a steep cliff but a gradual descent.
Before we realize it, we have altered or abandoned long-cherished
beliefs and doctrine. James Dolezal sounds the alarm on the important
but forgotten doctrine of divine simplicity. He calls the church back to
its traditional understanding and creedal affirmations not because he
fears change, but because they are biblical. This book is well worth the
time to read, digest, and reinvigorate our understanding of the simplicity of God."

— J. V. Fesko, Professor of Systematic and Historical
Theology, Westminster Seminary California

"Very few volumes of theology have stirred my profound intrigue as
James Dolezal's *All That Is in God*. The book describes the heart of
classical theology in its brilliant defense of the catholic view of the
nature and character of God. It also chronicles the contemporary drift
among some evangelical and Reformed scholars away from the orthodox understanding of God's simplicity and immutability. A must read."

— R. C. Sproul, Founder of Ligonier Ministries and
author of *The Holiness of God*.

"*All That Is in God: Evangelical Theology and the Challenge of Classical Christian Theism* offers an exceptionally clear, concise, and compelling presentation of what, until recently, catholic Christians have believed and confessed regarding the being and perfection of the triune God. It also offers incisive analysis of much contemporary evangelical teaching about God, concluding that both conservative and progressive 'theistic mutualists' share common assumptions and fallacies regarding the being and activity of God. I know of no other contemporary book that makes both of these contributions together in one place, and certainly not with the degree of clarity, charity, and persuasiveness that Dolezal's book exhibits. A worthy book that deserves a wide readership!"

—Scott R. Swain, President and James Woodrow Hassell
Professor of Systematic Theology,
Reformed Theological Seminary in Orlando

"*All That Is in God* is a fine sequel to the author's God without Parts (2011). The chapters provide an excellent guide to the main contours of classical theism. Dr. Dolezal also sounds a timely warning to those who have been tempted to modify this theism in the interests of what he aptly calls 'theistic mutualism.' The result is an excellent, up-to-date reminder of the Christian doctrine of God as understood by the conciliar statements and by the mainstream Reformed confessions."

—Paul Helm, Teaching Fellow, Regent College

ALL THAT IS IN GOD

ALL THAT IS IN GOD

*Evangelical Theology and the Challenge of
Classical Christian Theism*

James E. Dolezal

Reformation Heritage Books
Grand Rapids, Michigan

All That Is in God: Evangelical Theology and the Challenge of Classical Christian Theism
© 2017 by James E. Dolezal

Reformation Heritage Books
3070 29th St. SE
Grand Rapids, MI 49512
616-977-0889
orders@heritagebooks.org
www.heritagebooks.org

Printed in the United States of America
21 22 23 24 25/12 11 10 9 8 7 6 5

Library of Congress Cataloging-in-Publication Data

Names: Dolezal, James E., author.
Title: All that is in God : evangelical theology and the challenge of classical
    Christian theism / James E. Dolezal.
Description: Grand Rapids, Michigan : Reformation Heritage Books, 2017. |
    Includes bibliographical references and index.
Identifiers: LCCN 2017020519 (print) | LCCN 2017022147 (ebook) | ISBN
    9781601785558 (epub) | ISBN 9781601785541 (pbk. : alk. paper)
Subjects: LCSH: God (Christianity) | Theism—History of doctrines. |
    Reformed Church—Doctrines. | Evangelicalism.
Classification: LCC BT103 (ebook) | LCC BT103 .D65 2017 (print) | DDC
    231—dc23
LC record available at https://lccn.loc.gov/2017020519

For additional Reformed literature, request a free book list from Reformation Heritage Books at the above regular or e-mail address.

For my father,

Richard Dolezal,
the first to teach me the fear of the Lord and
the importance of sound doctrine

All that is in him is himself.

—JOHN OWEN

———⇒•◆•⇐———

Whatever is in God is the divine essence.

—THOMAS AQUINAS

———⇒•◆•⇐———

There is nothing accidental in God.

—AUGUSTINE OF HIPPO

Contents

Foreword

The statement that theology is at a crossroads could be applied to almost any moment in the history of Christian thought. To make that point as a general characterization of the present moment is, therefore, not to say anything new or even revolutionary. What matters, in each historical moment, is the road taken—and the road not taken. In the present moment, evangelical and Reformed theology has before it several different roads, one of which is the extension of those theological approaches that have served Christianity well during its many centuries, while others propose to take Christian doctrine down a series of specious alternative routes that purport to recast various doctrines in ways that seem more appealing to a largely rootless community of postmodern seekers-after-meaning.

Traditional understandings of God, both of the divine essence and attributes and of the Trinity, have been caricatured for the sake of replacing them with notions of a changing, temporal deity whose oneness is merely social. This social trinitarianism, often with tendencies toward subordinationism, has become a convenient tool kit for resolving issues in human society, and even the concept of perichoresis or coinherence (which was developed for the sake of explaining the inward threeness of the ultimate, spiritual, noncomposite, and unitary divine being) has been misappropriated into the mundane order by way of a confused Christian ethics. God is argued to take on new temporal attributes, and the Creator-creature relationship is described in panentheistic terms.

James Dolezal's *All That Is in God* offers an articulate analysis and critique of this series of problematic but fairly widely accepted developments in contemporary evangelical and Reformed theology. Dolezal's critiques are right on target, fair, remarkably readable, and measured. Even more importantly, his presentation of the doctrinal alternatives that belong to traditional Christian orthodoxy convincingly demonstrates the superiority of classical theism over the recently proposed alternatives.

Dolezal's criticisms of "mutualist" or "temporalist" understandings of God that have invaded evangelical thought provide a salutary warning against the aberrant argumentation of various recent writers who have taken incarnation as the basis of a claim that God takes on new attributes over the course of time, as if the union of the temporal human nature with the eternal divine nature imported temporality into God. Once incarnation is taken as a model for divine self-alteration, the notion of divine temporality is retrojected onto creation and becomes a basis for the claim that God adds new attributes to His nature in order to interact with creatures—in the case of one writer's mutualist speculations, the act of creation indicates a new "covenantal character"; namely, a series of new "properties" in God.

As Dolezal points out, the underlying problem of such argumentation is not only its rather unorthodox treatment of the incarnation and creation but its assumption that "a temporal effect can only proceed from a temporal act," even if the active agent is God (p. 96). The claim that God changes—taking on new attributes and changing in some respect in relation to creation or to human events without, however, being altered essentially—only makes sense when a series of traditionally orthodox assumptions concerning the doctrine of God are either removed from the picture or rendered unintelligible. The notion that God can be ontologically and ethically immutable at the same time that He has a "relational mutability" assumes—quite contrary to traditional orthodoxy—that changes in external relations imply a kind of mutability. As Dolezal points out, there is a clear antecedent to this kind of argumentation in the nineteenth-century "mediating theology" of Isaak Dorner, and that such argumentation yields divine mutability in the sense that God "begins to be what He was not by acquisition of real, new relations in Himself" as well as the conclusions that God is passible, composed of parts, finite, and temporally bound (p. 28).

The problem of composition in God carries over into what Dolezal identifies as "evangelical theistic mutualist" approaches to the Trinity. He points out that without a traditional doctrine of divine simplicity, the three divine persons become understood as "three discrete beings" (p. 105). Particularly telling is Dolezal's deflation of social trinitarianism, with its reduction of the unity of the Godhead to a social relationality, according to which "the Trinity is understood to be one thing, even if it is a complex thing consisting of persons, essences, and relations" (p. 126). This construct, which attempts to avoid the overt tritheism of Moltmann by claiming a generic divine essence, is "not," as Dolezal points out, "at all well suited to the maintenance of monotheism" (p. 127). (It is, by the way, a truism of classical monotheism that "God" is not a kind of being: whereas there is a genus "human," there is no genus "God.") The further social trinitarian argument that this social unity is based on the classic notion of perichoresis or mutual indwelling does not suffice to resolve the problem inasmuch as perichoresis is designed to explain the way in which the three persons participate in the one essence—not the way in which three distinct essences are socially interrelated.

At the heart of the modern aberrations, whether the invention of new divine attributes, the incipient tritheism of the social trinitarians, the notion of a somewhat mutable deity altered by relationality, or other variants on these contemporary themes is a radical misconstrual, whether intentional or unintentional, knowing or unknowing, of several of the traditional divine attributes, notably simplicity, immutability, and eternity, done in the name of divine relationality. What Dolezal provides is both a salutary critique and a clear, constructive argument for the superiority of classical Christian theism or, as I would prefer to call it, traditional Christian orthodoxy. He demonstrates that a traditional understanding of God included sound approaches to the doctrines of divine essence, attributes, and Trinity that accounted ably for the relationship between God and His creatures without compromising eternity, simplicity, and immutability—indeed, by offering a nuanced perspective on how these attributes actually frame and reinforce the doctrine of God. This is an important book. It deserves close attention from teachers, pastors, and students—indeed, from anyone confronted by the confused mass of misleading theologies put forth today under the guise of new and relevant reconstructions of the evangelical and Reformed faith.

Richard A. Muller

Preface

In this volume, I aim to acquaint readers with some of the fundamental claims of classical Christian theism and to commend these claims as nothing less than the truth about God as He has disclosed Himself in creation and in Holy Scripture. But this is also a polemical work. I endeavor to challenge certain doctrinal errors about God that have taken hold within the world of evangelical theology and even within much of modern Calvinism. Many of the views I critique in this volume are views I once held.

The chief problem I address in this work is the abandonment of God's simplicity and of the infinite pure actuality of His being. I suspect that many Christians make this mistake unwittingly because they have never considered what is involved in those traditional doctrines. This was certainly true for me. Others, however, are knowingly hostile to the traditional doctrines. It is not uncommon to read modern theologians, even many Calvinists, who disparage these older teachings as the unfortunate residue of Greek philosophy. In their estimation, the sooner we dispense with such vain speculations and get back to our Bibles, the better.

But having discarded doctrines such as divine simplicity and pure actuality, we find that we can no longer read the Bible the way most Christians historically read it. In particular, when the Scripture portrays God as changing in relation to His creatures, this would no longer be understood as an accommodation of His revelation to us but rather as an accommodation of His being. Any newness in God's works in the created order is thought to signal a movement of some sort in His very being, just as some change takes place in humans when we undertake new actions. This seems to make God genuinely relational and personal in a give-and-take way. Divine simplicity and pure actuality are no longer employed in ruling out such mutualistic understandings of the God-world relation. In order not to entirely lose the doctrines articulated in the ecumenical creeds and Reformed confessions, many have suggested that these changes are somehow situated in God alongside His unchanging essence. This approach is thought to preserve the best of both the classical and mutualistic perspectives: God as being and God as becoming.

But can such an arrangement really work? I am convinced it cannot. And the reason is that, because He is simple and purely actual, God is not capable of receiving new determinations or features of being—not even if He sovereignly chooses to. Any change in God, even a nonessential one, would introduce new being or actuality into Him. The Christian who believes that God experiences a change of any sort is no longer able to say with the older theologians, "All that is in God is God." He instead conceives that God's being is a mixture of divinity and the new qualities of being by which His divinity has been augmented. From the viewpoint of classical Christian orthodoxy, such outcomes are unacceptable, for they undermine the very absoluteness of God's life and existence and so, by extension, the believer's utter reliance upon God.

Perhaps it is fitting to say a word or two about sources and method. Our Reformed orthodox forefathers freely and skillfully deployed patristic and medieval Catholic sources in their defense of the classical doctrine of God. In keeping with their approach, I have sought to utilize helpful authors, both old and new, Catholic and Protestant, insofar as these uphold biblical and classical Christian orthodoxy on the points under consideration. This no more signals an endorsement of Roman Catholicism than a Roman Catholic's agreement with a Protestant author on a given point indicates an endorsement of Protestantism.

As for method, it is possible that the discussion in this volume will be more philosophical in character than that to which many readers are accustomed. In some respects, this is unavoidable, as the matters being considered have historically been treated with the assistance of philosophical concepts. These concepts allow us to speak more precisely than would otherwise be possible. As with any discipline, the proper terminology must be learned if one is to enter more fully into the discussions concerning that field of knowledge. An attempt is made to clarify difficult or technical terminology, and I trust that even those unfamiliar with such vocabulary will nevertheless be able to follow the main threads of argumentation.

Additionally, the method of this work is that of contemplative theology. The contemplative approach to theology has been somewhat obscured in recent history by the rise of biblical theology as a specialized method of theological inquiry. These two approaches to Christian doctrine need not be in conflict. I readily affirm that biblical theology has been a profound catalyst for improving and enriching our understanding of the progress of redemption. But it seems to me that biblical theology, with its unique focus on historical development and progress, is not best suited for the study of theology proper. The reason for this is because God is not a historical individual, and neither does His intrinsic activity undergo development or change. This places God beyond the proper focus of biblical theology. God is not changed by what He does—though what He does certainly brings about progress in history, creatures, and salvation. In an attempt to understand God as one of the historical characters in the narrative of redemption, many have fallen into the trap of historicizing His very life and existence. Suffice it to say, while biblical theology tells us many true things about God, its proper focus on development and progress is not methodologically suitable to the study of the One who does not change.

The contemplative approach to theology proper treats God as an ahistorical being and seeks to discover the timeless truths about Him by thinking through the implications and entailments of those things He has revealed to us in creation and Scripture (and this certainly includes those things revealed about God in the unfolding course of redemptive history). It proceeds in a logical way from major premises through minor premises to conclusions. Sometimes these conclusions involve denials, such as the disavowal of body, parts, and passions in God. At other times the conclusions are more positive, such as affirming God's omnipotence, pure actuality, self-subsistence, or absoluteness. This volume is full of both affirmations and denials arrived at via contemplation.

In setting forth this volume, it is my hope and prayer that others may be helped to perceive the harmful theological implications of reconceiving God as one who derives aspects of His life or being from His creatures. It is not my intent to question the sincere love for God exhibited by those I critique; neither is it to impugn their persons. It is rather to identify a pattern of unsound words that has regrettably emerged and to aid readers in returning to the older paths of theological orthodoxy, the paths in which God is more truly glorified as God.

Acknowledgments

The substance of this volume has been adapted from a series of lectures delivered at the Southern California Reformed Baptist Pastors' Conference held at Trinity Reformed Baptist Church in La Mirada, California, in November 2015. I am grateful to Richard Barcellos for his invitation to speak at the conference and for his encouragement to develop my lectures into a volume for publication. Without his prodding, much of what is contained here would never have been written. Samuel and Kimberly Renihan were excellent hosts during my time in La Mirada, providing refreshment and wonderful opportunities for fellowship and theological discussion in their home.

Many people have aided me in thinking though the issues discussed in this book. Paul Helm supplied thoughtful feedback on drafts of each chapter. His insight and friendship have been an immense blessing to me. Jonathan Master and Richard Dolezal also provided helpful evaluations of the original lecture notes that eventually evolved into this monograph. Deryck Barson gave useful suggestions for my chapter on the Trinity, and Robert LaRocca has been my constant dialogue partner on the topics discussed in this book for more than seven years. Scott Swain's enthusiasm for this work and his willingness to use an earlier draft of it with his students has been an encouragement to me. Jay Collier and Ryan Hurd of Reformation Heritage Books provided excellent editorial guidance and recommendations.

Most of all, I would like to thank my wife Courtney and our children, Judah, Havah, and Eden, for the many sacrifices they made to enable me to undertake this study and the preparation of this volume. Their love is one of God's greatest benedictions to me.

CHAPTER 1

Models of Theism

Two distinctly different models of Christian theism are presently vying for the heart and mind of evangelical Christianity. The approach of classical Christian theism is what one discovers in older Protestant confessions such as the Belgic Confession, Thirty-Nine Articles of Religion, Westminster Confession of Faith, and Second London Confession of Faith. This approach is basically in keeping with the view of God as found in the works of patristic and medieval Christian theologians such as Athanasius, Augustine, Anselm, and Aquinas. It is marked by a strong commitment to the doctrines of divine aseity, immutability, impassibility, simplicity, eternity, and the substantial unity of the divine persons. The underlying and inviolable conviction is that God does not derive any aspect of His being from outside Himself and is not in any way caused to be.

In contrast to this older view of a radically independent, simple, and purely actual God stands the newer approach of theistic mutualism,[1] called by some "theistic personalism."[2] In an effort to portray God as

---

1. "Mutualism," as I am using the term, denotes a symbiotic relationship in which both parties derive something from each other. In such a relation, it is requisite that each party be capable of being ontologically moved or acted upon and thus determined by the other. This does not necessarily require parity between the parties involved. Accordingly, a mutualistic relation could obtain even if only one of the parties involved were the architect and ultimate regulator of the relation.

2. The label "theistic personalism" appears to be the coinage of Brian Davies. See *An Introduction to the Philosophy of Religion*, 3rd ed. (Oxford: Oxford University Press, 2004), 2–16. I have chosen to use the term "mutualism" instead of "personalism" simply for the sake of clarity. Davies's objection to theistic personalism is at its heart an objection to the mutualism that seems to be entailed in all univocist understandings

more relatable, theistic mutualists insist that God is involved in a genuine give-and-take relationship with His creatures. Theistic mutualists
may disagree among themselves on precisely how much control God
has over the give-and-take process, but all agree that God is somehow
involved in such an exchange. Edward Feser explains that the proponent of this newer theistic outlook ordinarily "objects to the notion of
God as immutable, impassible, and eternal—finding it too cold and
otherworldly, and incompatible with a literal reading of various biblical passages—and typically has philosophical objections to the notion
of divine simplicity."[3] Feser identifies modern philosophers such as
Alvin Plantinga and Richard Swinburne as advocates of this approach.
Theistic mutualism is committed to univocal thinking and speaking
with regard to God and the world and thus conceives God as interact-
ing with the world in some way like humans do, even if on a much
grander scale.[4]

The orbit of theistic mutualism extends well beyond the realm
of philosophy. It also appears in the writings of several evangelical
theologians, perhaps most conspicuously in those of the open theist

---

of the term "person." David Bentley Hart calls the mutualist conception of God
"monopolytheism" since, as he explains,

> it seems to involve a view of God not conspicuously different from the poly-
> theistic picture of the gods as merely very powerful discrete entities who
> possess a variety of distinct attributes that lesser entities also possess, if in
> smaller measure; it differs from polytheism…solely in that it posits the exis-
> tence of only one such being. It is a way of thinking that suggests that God,
> since he is only a particular instantiation of various concepts and properties,
> is logically dependent on some more comprehensive reality embracing both
> him and other beings.

The Experience of God: Being, Consciousness, Bliss (New Haven, Conn.: Yale University Press, 2013), 127–28. Hart rightly characterizes, in my opinion, what is inevitably
involved in all univocist views of God.

3. Edward Feser, "Classical Theism," Edward Feser (blog), September 30, 2010,
http://edwardfeser.blogspot.com/2010/09/classical-theism.html.

4. Univocist approaches to thinking and speaking about God necessarily conceive
of God's being as existing (in some respect) within the same order of being as that of
creatures and thus as existentially correlative to them. A God who can be moved or
affected by His creatures, even if only in accord with His choice to be so moved or
affected, is such a God.

persuasion.[5] Less obvious perhaps is how deeply theistic mutualism has taken root in the thinking of many who adhere to the older Protestant confessions. Theologians within the various confessional branches of evangelicalism—usually Calvinists—have been among the most vociferous opponents of openness theology, in particular with regard to the question of divine exhaustive foreknowledge.[6] Nevertheless, many of them share with open and process theists the theistic mutualist belief that God's being is such that He is capable of being moved by His creatures. There are undoubtedly many reasons for this adherence to theistic mutualism among modern evangelical Calvinists, and it is not my purpose in this volume to investigate each of these reasons. Suffice it to say that confessional Calvinists who uphold any aspect of theistic mutualism are faced with the peculiar and perhaps insurmountable challenge of reconciling their mutualist understanding of the God-world relation with the language and intent of the classical Reformed creeds.

It should be noted that there are both hard and soft versions of theistic mutualism. The harder sort regards God as a person who allows other beings to function as first causes or absolute originators of actions, events, or objects and who Himself stands as an onlooker within creation, susceptible to an increase in knowledge. Hard theistic mutualism also tends to regard God as needing the world in some respect; thus, He is compelled to create and sustain it. It is this harder theistic mutualism that is espoused by open theists and process theists. Soft theistic mutualism, in contrast, tends to hold that God does not create the world by dint of absolute necessity; neither does He need the world in any significant sense. Moreover, many soft theistic mutualists do not believe that God is intellectually open or in process of development. Indeed, many who subscribe to the softer

---

5. See Clark Pinnock et al., *The Openness of God: A Biblical Challenge to the Traditional Understanding of God* (Downers Grove, Ill.: IVP, 1994). See also Clark H. Pinnock, *Most Moved Mover: A Theology of God's Openness* (Grand Rapids: Baker Academic, 2001).

6. See, for example, Bruce A. Ware, "Defining Evangelicalism's Boundaries Theologically: Is Open Theism Evangelical?", *Journal of the Evangelical Theological Society* 45 (June 2002): 193–212.

variety of mutualism have stood firmly against intellectual and volitional "becoming" in God. They maintain that God neither learns
nor depends on creation for His knowledge and that His will is not
changed by the actions of creatures. Nevertheless, they do allow for
a measure of ontological becoming and process in God. This is to the
extent that they—along with the harder theistic mutualists—insist
that God undergoes changes in relation and in those alleged intellectual
and emotive states of His that are thought to correlate to His changing relations with creatures. This ontological openness to being changed
by creatures, whether initiated by God or by creatures themselves, is
the common denominator in all forms of theistic mutualism. Theistic
mutualists may disagree among themselves on precisely how much process and development to allow in God or even over what the ultimate
source or cause of such development might be. But all hold to a divine
ontology that allows for God to acquire and shed actuality of being.

At first glance, the moniker "theistic mutualism" (or "theistic personalism") seems harmless enough. Perhaps it is even attractive insofar
as orthodox Christians believe in a God who subsists as three persons
in relation and who lovingly calls us into the joy of personal fellowship
with Him.[7] No doubt patristic, medieval, Reformation, and Puritan
theologians held forth the glorious prospect of the sinner's reconciliation to God and the benediction of unbroken fellowship with Him
in glory. Theistic mutualists recognize that classical Christian theists
believe such things. They are not convinced, however, that the traditional emphasis upon a wholly unchanging, simple, and purely actual
God is sufficient to deliver such blessings to us. They think that if God
cannot change or be affected by the world in any way, then our relationship to Him seems overly one-sided and thus rather impersonal
and nondynamic. Furthermore, the Bible depicts God as ensconced
within our history as one whose relationship with humans plays
out along the same temporal lines as relationships between human
persons—loving and merciful at one moment (Ex. 3:7–9), grieved and
angry at another (Ex. 32:9–10; Ezek. 16:42–43), turning away from

---

7. See John 3:16; 17:3, 21; and 1 John 1:3: "And truly our fellowship is with the
Father and with His Son Jesus Christ."

man and returning to man in mercy and reconciliation (Ex. 32:14; Ps. 80:19; Mal. 3:7). These are the components that make personal relationships truly personal, are they not? From the viewpoint of theistic mutualism, such dynamic reciprocity and mutuality seem to call for an overhaul of the well-intentioned, if misguided, classical emphasis upon a God who cannot change in any way whatsoever. Intended to replace the older strong account of an absolutely unchangeable God, the newer doctrine makes space for mutual give-and-take with God in an interpersonal way. The nineteenth-century German Lutheran theologian Isaak August Dorner expresses this revisionist outlook with pointed clarity:

> We will have to teach the following: that not only does humanity change in its relation to God, but the living relations of God to humanity…also undergo changes, as both are manifest in the world. And if we establish this point, then the concept of God is not merely the wooden concept of the highest being, but the vital absolute personality that stands in a living relation of mercy and love to the life of the worlds and its changing needs and conditions. Without reciprocity between God and world such vital relations would have no authentic reality.[8]

Dorner is particularly insistent that for God to stand in an authentic, loving relation to the world, He must be open to human action and influence upon Him. He continues, "It is also to be said further that the relation of love between God and man must be a *reciprocal relation*, as this is required by the nature of love. Consequently, it is to be taught that God *himself*, who on the side of generating power remains eternally the sole original principle, enters the realm of the ethical or love in a reciprocal relation; yes, *God enters into a relation of mutual and reciprocal influence*."[9]

But should the newer ideal of a mutually interactive, give-and-take relationship with God be allowed to eclipse or adjust the claims of classical Christian theism? The concern from the classical perspective

---

8. Isaak August Dorner, *Divine Immutability: A Critical Reconsideration*, trans. Robert R. Williams and Claude Welch (Minneapolis: Fortress Press, 1994), 110.

9. Dorner, *Divine Immutability*, 148.

is that theistic mutualists have made human personal relations, which are irreducibly correlative, the paradigm for understanding all meaningful relations. To the extent that theistic mutualists believe God to exist in such a relationship with the world, they appear to undermine His perfection and fullness of being. In short, God has been reconceived as deriving some aspects of His being in correlation with the world, and this can be nothing less than a depredation of His fullness of life and existential absoluteness.

Some adherents to the classical view regard the mutualist account of the God-world relation as advancing an idolatrous form of theism insomuch as it locates the being of God inescapably within the order of finite beings, even if it still affirms that He is the greatest being in that order. The Anglican theologian E. L. Mascall argues that a God who derives any actuality of His being from His creatures—which the God of theistic mutualism necessarily does—could not possibly be the first cause of all creation. This is because He would "provide a foundation neither for himself nor for anything else." Mascall concludes, "Unless we are prepared to accept the God of classical theism, we may as well be content to do without a God at all."[10] Catholic theologian Herbert McCabe notifies us that "there has been a deplorable and idolatrous tendency on the part of some Christians to diminish God. In order that God may *stand in relationship* with his creatures, he is made one of them, a member of the universe, subject to change and even disappointment and suffering."[11] He deems this mutualist understanding to be a "false and idolatrous picture of God" because it unavoidably considers Him to be "an inhabitant of the universe, existing alongside his creatures."[12] More recently, the Eastern Orthodox scholar David Bentley Hart has insisted that any proposed alternative to the God of classical theism "can never be more than an idol: a god, but not God; a *theos*, but not *ho Theos*; a being, not Being in its transcendent

---

10. E. L. Mascall, *He Who Is: A Study in Traditional Theism* (London: Longmans, Green, 1943), 96.

11. Herbert McCabe, *God Matters* (London: Geoffrey Chapman, 1987), 18. Emphasis original.

12. McCabe, *God Matters*, 11.

fullness."[13] The reason for these strong objections to mutualist understandings of God is that such a God is inevitably mutable and finite and as such is unworthy of worship. This unhappy verdict is not meant to attack the intentions of theistic mutualists. Many seem to have been unwittingly caught up into the mutualistic way of thinking about God, wholly unaware of its idolatrous implications.

In the chapters that follow, I aim to spotlight the conflict between the classical and mutualist perspectives on God by examining some of the significant doctrinal flashpoints—most notably, divine immutability, simplicity, eternity, and substantial unity. Not all of the theistic mutualists with whom I engage are equally at odds with these various tenets of classical orthodoxy, and indeed, many believe themselves to be in basic agreement with these dogmas. As I hope to make clear, this agreement is often more imagined than real and frequently follows from a misunderstanding of the genuine meaning and implications of the classical doctrines. It is not uncommon nowadays, for instance, to encounter claims that God is both immutable and mutable, both impassible and passible, both simple and complex, both timeless and temporal, and so forth. This newfound proclivity for a dualistic both/and approach to theism is particularly fashionable among modern Calvinist theologians who for various reasons dislike the strictures of classical theism but are unwilling to embrace the more radical position of open theism or some other form of process theism. Arguably, however, such theologians have already embraced a rudimentary form of process theism to the extent that they allow some measure of ontological becoming and dependency in God.

Part of the reason many evangelical theistic mutualists do not recognize that they have already adopted a form of ontological becoming in God is because they have lost sight of what "being" means. They mistakenly assume that "being" indicates merely "nature" or "essence." Rather, it denotes any actuality or "is-ness" whatsoever, that is, any participation in the act of existing (in *esse*, or "to be").[14] If God should not

---

13. Hart, *Experience of God*, 250.

14. Etienne Gilson contrasts the essentialist understanding of being with its true existential meaning. Philosophy and theology continue to be plagued by ignoring the

be all that He is in and of Himself infinitely and eternally, then He would no longer be pure and simple being but rather becoming, and thus dependent on that which supplies new actuality to Him.

Such a conception of God must not go unchallenged if we are to be true to Holy Scripture and to the faithful explication of Scripture's meaning as it has been handed down to us in the various conciliar statements and Reformed confessions. It is the desire to rehabilitate a robust understanding of God's ontological absoluteness that motivates this volume. For Calvinists in particular, this work is twofold. Negatively, it requires that we identify and abandon those newer doctrinal constructions whereby God's being has been relativized. Positively, it requires the rehabilitation of the catholic orthodoxy of the older Reformed confessions and theologians, particularly with respect to the understanding of God's actuality. The chapters that follow by no means approach the magnitude of this task, but are offered simply as a beginning to that much-needed work.

---

deeper existential sense of "being." See *Being and Some Philosophers*, 2nd ed. (Toronto: Pontifical Institute of Mediaeval Studies, 1952). See also Joseph Owens, *An Interpretation of Existence* (Milwaukee, Wis.: Bruce, 1968). For a comprehensive study of being as it would have been understood by Thomas Aquinas and many of the Protestant scholastics who followed him, see John F. Wippel, *The Metaphysical Thought of Thomas Aquinas: From Finite Being to Uncreated Being* (Washington, D.C.: Catholic University of America Press, 2000).

CHAPTER 2

Unchanging God

Does God change? Perhaps no question more clearly illuminates the conflict between the older teaching of classical Christian theism and the newer commitments of theistic mutualism. Open theists and process theists generally contend that divine immutability suggests imperfection in God. The thinking is that ability to change is better than being unable to change. Thus, a perfect God must be changeable in some significant ways. Process theist Burton Z. Cooper claims that "the perfection of God lies in the quality of the relative response rather than in the priority of the (absolute) act."[1] He questions the traditional "assumption that perfection excludes passivity." In order to avoid completely losing the continuity of God's identity, process theists regard Him as comprised of two aspects of being: one absolute and the other relative. Charles Hartshorne explains that "God…is in one aspect of his being strictly or maximally absolute, and in another aspect no less strictly or maximally relative."[2] Such dipolarity is designed to allow God's identity both to remain constant and to be subject to genuine process and development, especially in the context of a relationship with beings outside of Himself.

While there is a strong affinity for process theism among open theists, evangelical Calvinists in contrast have been at the vanguard in repudiating these newer theisms. This makes it all the more remarkable

---

1. Burton Z. Cooper, *The Idea of God: A Whiteheadian Critique of St. Thomas Aquinas' Concept of God* (The Hague: Martinus Nijhoff, 1974), 94.

2. Charles Hartshorne, *The Divine Relativity: A Social Conception of God* (New Haven, Conn.: Yale University Press, 1948), 32.

that so many recent evangelical Calvinists seem to endorse a similar divine ontology to that of open and process theism. In particular, it seems that the belief that there is both absolute and relative actuality in God is no longer unique to process theists. Many recent Calvinists advance their own version of the absolute-relative distinction by distinguishing between God's essence, which is said not to change, and other contingent—thus, "relative"—aspects of His being. It is in the contingent aspects of His being in which He undergoes changes. Where these Calvinistic theologians tend to differ from process and open theists is simply with regard to the source and scope of change they allow in God. This newfound willingness on the part of many Calvinists to permit a measure of mutability in God is perhaps most accentuated in their unfavorable judgment of the classical doctrine of divine impassibility.

In what follows, I will first briefly articulate the older view of God's self-sufficiency and immutability together with a few remarks on how the tradition accounts for biblical depictions of God as undergoing change. Second, I will set forth the theistic mutualist claims of some select modern Calvinists, with special attention given to the diminishment of divine immutability. Third, I will address the question of whether reconceiving divine sovereignty as a power God exercises over His very being is sufficient to forestall the potential problems of a weakened doctrine of immutability. Finally, I will consider what is at stake if the classical doctrine of God's immutability is softened.

The Self-Sufficient and Unchanging God of Classical Theism

Classical Christian theism is deeply devoted to the absoluteness of God with respect to His existence, essence, and activity. Nothing about God's being is derived or caused to be. There is nothing behind Him or outside Him that could increase, alter, or augment His infinite fullness of being and felicity. For this reason, He cannot subject Himself to changes because every change involves a cause that brings to the subject an actuality of being that the subject lacks in and of itself. Causes, simply put, make things to be. Therefore, if God is wholly uncaused and self-sufficient in the plentitude of His being, then He cannot be moved to some further actuality. This would suggest some imperfection or absence of being and goodness in Him.

Divine Aseity and Pure Actuality

The perfection that maintains God's self-sufficiency is sometimes referred to as God's aseity (from the Latin *a se*—of himself, from himself). Herman Bavinck explains the significance of this doctrine: "When God ascribes this aseity to himself in Scripture, he makes himself known as absolute being, as the one who *is* in an absolute sense. By this perfection he is at once essentially and absolutely distinct from all creatures."[3] The English Puritan Stephen Charnock makes a similar point regarding aseity: "God is of himself, from no other.... God hath no original; he hath no defect because he was not made of nothing: he hath no increase because he had no beginning. He was before all things, and, therefore, depends upon no other thing."[4] That which has no beginning cannot begin to be in any respect. One clear implication of this doctrine is that God neither derives anything from His creation, nor is He the cause of Himself: "It is evident from the word 'aseity,' God is exclusively from himself, not in the sense of being self-caused but being from eternity to eternity who he is, being not becoming."[5] This doctrine is supported by a number of biblical passages.

In Job 22:2–3, Job's friend Eliphaz challenges Job with a set of rhetorical questions:

> Can a man be profitable to God,
> Though he who is wise may be profitable to himself?
> Is it any pleasure to the Almighty that you are righteous?
> Or is it gain to Him that you make your ways blameless?

---

3. Herman Bavinck, *Reformed Dogmatics*, ed. John Bolt, trans. John Vriend (Grand Rapids: Baker Academic, 2004), 2:152. For a fine, recent discussion of this doctrine, see John Webster, "Life in and of Himself: Reflections on God's Aseity," in *Engaging the Doctrine of God: Contemporary Protestant Perspectives*, ed. Bruce L. McCormack (Grand Rapids: Baker Academic, 2008), 107–24.

4. Stephen Charnock, *The Existence and Attributes of God* (1853; repr., Grand Rapids: Baker, 1979), 1:321.

5. Bavinck, *Reformed Dogmatics*, 2:152.

The thrust of these questions is that God is not obligated to man because God cannot receive anything from him. God is not a little better or worse off because of us. We add nothing to Him and deduct nothing from Him. John Calvin makes this point in a sermon on this passage:

> For we bring him no gain and he is made neither hot nor cold (as I say) by us: and as we can do him no good, so also we can do him no harm.... For we imagine that God might receive some commodity by us, as though he had need of us. But contrariwise, he can neither increase nor diminish: he is in such sort the fountain of all goodness, that he will borrow nothing of another man, and that which men bring unto him, is not to relieve his necessity, or augment him in anywise.... Now if any men would ask the question, wherefore then doth God require of us, that we should be diligent to serve him? It seems that he hath some respect to himself. No: there is no consideration but of us, and of our salutation: God hath no respect of his own profit, when he gives us the rule of good living, and commands us to abstain from evil, and requires us to do this or that.... He considers what is good for us and expedient for our salvation.... As for God, he remains always safe and sound. It is true that (as much as lies in us) we offend his Majesty, abolish his justice, and are guilty thereof. Yet it cannot be said that we diminish anything of God, or that we can rob him of that which he has, or that we can reach unto him, to do him any injury. No truly.[6]

In Job 35:6–7, Eliphaz's charge is repeated by the young man Elihu:

If you sin, what do you accomplish against Him?
Or, if your transgressions are multiplied,
    what do you do to Him?
If you are righteous, what do you give Him?
Or what does He receive from your hand?

---

6. John Calvin, *Sermons of Master John Calvin upon the Book of Job*, trans. Arthur Golding (London: Impensis Georgij Bishop, 1574; repr., Edinburgh: Banner of Truth Trust, 1993), 389. Throughout the use of this source, I have updated the spelling.

Calvin expounds upon the aseity of God from this passage: "But we must apply this doctrine to the present intent of Elihu: which is, that God is not like mortal men, which are moved and touched. And why? Because they have need of another's help, and cannot set light by [i.e., disregard] other men's force. Thus you see what the cause is that we be moved and carried to and fro. But there must no such dotages enter into our head concerning God."[7]

In the context of the Job narrative, both these rebukes of Eliphaz and Elihu are in response to Job's insistence that he is righteous and that God thus owes him a hearing and an explanation regarding the calamity that has come upon him (see Job 31:33–37). The two rebukes imply that God owes no one anything because He receives nothing from the creature. God is not touched or moved by His creation inasmuch as touching or moving conveys new actuality to the one touched or moved and thus indebts the one moved to the mover.

Lest we conclude that all this is merely the unsound counsel of Job's misguided friends, we should consider God's own words in Job 41:11, as they bear a striking similarity to those of Job's friends: "Who has preceded Me, that I should pay him? Everything under heaven is Mine." The Hebrew term for "preceded" (קִדְּמַנִי) could also be translated "confronted" or "come to be in front of." The idea is that no one has gotten out in front of God or gotten the upper hand on Him by giving something to Him so that He is now indebted or obligated to that person (see Paul's citation of Job 41:11 in Romans 11:35). The reason God can receive nothing from us is because we have nothing to give Him that He does not already possess. When God gives to His creatures, He does not give away—that is, He does not divest Himself of being and actuality when He gives good gifts to humans. Consequently, we have nothing to bestow on God that He does not already perfectly and infinitely possess in His fullness of being. As we cannot subtract from His infinite beatitude, neither can we replenish or enlarge it.

---

7. Calvin, *Sermons on Job*, 642. In these sermons, Calvin emphasizes God as the source of all being who Himself cannot be moved by His creatures.

Another important text for establishing God's aseity and perfect self-sufficiency is Acts 17:23b–28. In the context, the apostle Paul is confronting the idolatry and ignorance of the Athenians.

> Therefore, the One whom you worship without knowing, Him I proclaim to you: "God, who made the world and everything in it, since He is Lord of heaven and earth, does not dwell in temples made with hands. Nor is He worshiped with men's hands, as though He needed anything, since He gives to all life, breath, and all things. And He has made from one blood every nation of men to dwell on all the face of the earth, and has determined their preappointed times and the boundaries of their dwellings, so that they should seek the Lord, in the hope that they might grope for Him and find Him, though He is not far from each one of us; for in Him we live and move and have our being, as also some of your own poets have said, 'For we are also His offspring.'"

After appropriating the language of Solomon that God does not dwell in temples made with hands (1 Kings 8:27), Paul informs his Athenian interlocutors that God is not served by human hands as though He needed anything. The reason we do not give to Him is because He is the one who gives to all life, breath, and all things and thus receives from none. Moreover, we live and move and have our being in Him. If this is the case, then there cannot be some actuality of being that we possess and God lacks. Again, God's giving to us of all these things does not entail divine divestment such that when we "serve" Him with those gifts He is somehow enriched or repaid by our actions.

God's glory is not actually increased when we glorify Him. His perfect fullness of love is not intensified by our acts of obedience. His intrinsic, infinite hatred for sin is not made a little hotter by our transgressions. All these things—being glorious, loving, opposed to sin—God simply *is* in and of Himself. The delight He manifests in repentant sinners and the wrath He reveals against the ungodly are nothing but His own fullness of perfect being variously disclosed with reference to particular creatures at different times (see Psalm 18:25–27). Man is not the agent by which these actualities are produced in God.

Human actions are simply the occasions for the unfolding of God's *ad extra* display of these unchanging and unacquired virtues.

God's aseity also entails that He is perfect and purely actual in being. Because He depends on nothing outside Himself, one can only conclude that God simply is that act of existence by which He is. Classical theists insist that God is being, not becoming. He has no passive potentiality or capacity by which He might become more or other than He is. This means that even His relation to the world as its Creator and Sustainer does not produce any new actuality in Him. One of the better known arguments for God's pure actuality appears in Thomas Aquinas's demonstration that God as first cause is the "Unmoved Mover." In summarizing his five ways for proving God's existence in his *Summa theologiae*, Thomas establishes that the first efficient cause of being must itself be pure act.[8] He contends that anything in motion (broadly conceived as anything that changes whatsoever) must have previously been in passive potency to that motion and thus moved to that motion by some source of actuality external to itself. As Thomas states, "Nothing can be reduced from potentiality to actuality, except by something in a state of actuality." Nothing can be made actual except by something already actual. Furthermore, it is "impossible that in the same respect and in the same way a thing should be both mover and moved, *i.e.*, that it should move itself." An external agent already in act is required for the reduction of potency to act. Anything put in motion (i.e., anything previously in passive potency) is put in motion by another and, as Thomas notes, "that by another again."[9] But this chain of movers cannot go on infinitely, or there would be no first mover—that is, no ultimately sufficient reason for movement.[10] Since

8. Thomas Aquinas, *Summa theologiae* Ia.2.3, in translation as *Summa Theologica*, trans. Fathers of the English Dominican Province (Allen, Tex.: Christian Classics, 1981).

9. Aquinas, *Summa theologiae* Ia.2.3.

10. Aquinas's argument is not that God is the first cause or mover in a mere chronological sense but rather that He is the first inasmuch as He is the most fundamental source and explanation of contingent being wherever and whenever it is found. This understanding of Aquinas's claim controverts the old accusation that his Five Ways teach that God is the first link on the great chain of being with creatures and thus stands univocally with them in the same order of being. See the discussion in Brian Davies,

the first mover is necessarily unmoved by another, and since all movement comes from some mover in act, that first mover must be pure act (*actus purus*). That is to say, God, as the first cause of all things, must be a being who is not susceptible to further actualization because He possesses fullness of being in and of Himself.

Pure actuality is understood by Thomists and the Reformed orthodox to be a necessary implication of divine aseity. Steven J. Duby explains the reasoning in this connection:

> Divine aseity entails…that God is *actus purus*. If God is entirely *a se* with no one and nothing back of him to account for him, then he is without causal susceptibility—without being moved or, indeed, a capacity to be moved—and therefore without the root of such causal susceptibility, namely, passive potency…. Aseity inflected as independence or *primitas* thus implies that God is fully in act. [11]

That which is pure act is dynamic and utterly full of being and life. Thus, it is entirely self-sufficient and independent of all others. John Owen picks up this same theme of God's pure actuality when he speaks of God's perfect and infinite fullness of being as the One in whom there is no principle of nonbeing—that is, no passive potency:

> God alone hath all being in him. Hence he gives himself the name, "I AM," Exod. iii.14. He was eternally All; when all things else that were made, or now are, or shall be, were nothing…. In this state of infinite, eternal being and goodness, antecedent unto any act of wisdom or power without himself to give existence unto other things, God was, and is, eternally in himself all that he will be, all that he can be, unto eternity. For where there is infinite being and infinite goodness, there is infinite blessedness and happiness, whereunto nothing can be added. God is always the same…. All things that are, make no addition unto God, no

---

Thomas Aquinas's Summa Theologiae: *A Guide and Commentary* (New York: Oxford University Press, 2014), 34–50. See also Richard A. Muller, "The Dogmatic Function of St. Thomas''Proofs': A Protestant Appreciation," *Fides et Historia* 24 (1992): 15–29.

11. Steven J. Duby, *Divine Simplicity: A Dogmatic Account* (London: Bloomsbury T&T Clark, 2016), 121.

change in his state. His blessedness, happiness, self-satisfaction, as well as all his other infinite perfections, were absolutely the same before the creation of anything.[12]

Far from suggesting some sort of impoverished isolationism, divine aseity and independence, as functions of God's pure actuality, actually speak of God's perfect blessedness, to which nothing can be added.

Divine Immutability

God's aseity and pure actuality naturally lead to a consideration of His immutability. Stephen Charnock declares, "He who hath not being from another, cannot but be always what he is: God is the first Being, an independent Being; he was not produced of himself, or of any other, but by nature always hath been, and, therefore, cannot by himself, or by any other, be changed from what he is in his own nature."[13] If there is nothing in God's existence or life that is given to Him by the creature, and if He is not the cause of Himself because He is pure being, then it follows that He cannot undergo change. That is, He cannot be made to be in any way that He is not in and of Himself already. If such should occur, one would have to explain how new actuality was made to appear in the being of God.[14] One would also have to say that the

---

12. John Owen, *The Glory of Christ*, in *The Works of John Owen*, ed. William Goold (1850–1853; repr., Edinburgh: Banner of Truth Trust, 1999), 1:368.

13. Charnock, *Existence and Attributes*, 1:319. It is not uncommon to encounter the accusation that the God of classical theism, such as Aquinas's Unmoved Mover, is somehow lifeless, cold, and static. Dorner makes this allegation: "The divine could not be living, but could only be rigid dead substance or equally lifeless law, if it were motionless in itself, without real distinction of the positing and posited life." *Divine Immutability*, 137. Against Dorner, we should observe that in fact the very opposite is the case. The God of classical theism is not unmoved because He lacks actuality and dynamism, but because He is *pure* unbounded act and dynamism and thus cannot be moved to some additional state of actuality, power, or liveliness. As pure act, God is life itself—*ipsa vita*.

14. God cannot give being to Himself since He cannot give what He does not have; and if He already possesses the fullness of being, He cannot receive it from Himself. No one is enriched in any way by what one already possesses. Such a notion of giving and receiving that of which one is already in perfect possession is trivial at best and nonsensical at worst. Enrichment requires addition of actuality. God can have nothing added to Him because He lacks no perfection of being and actuality.

agent who gave to God what He lacked had somehow "gotten out in front of God" (per the language of Job 41:11) and that God was now indebted or obligated to that agent. The immutable God may commit to bring about certain blessings or curses on His creatures via covenant (see, for example, Deuteronomy 11:26–28; 1 Kings 2:3–4; Isaiah 1:18–20), but this is not to be considered as God's placing Himself in a position in which He depends on His creatures or receives anything from their hands. God is not voluntarily subjecting Himself to being moved by His human covenantal counterparts when He makes certain promises or sets down certain conditions and stipulations.[15] As Wilhelmus à Brakel states, "No one can add to or subtract anything from his being, neither can anyone increase or decrease His felicity."[16]

Numerous biblical passages witness to God's unchangeableness. In Numbers 23:19, God does not repent; in Malachi 3:6, God says, "For I am the LORD, I do not change"; in James 1:17, God is "the Father of lights, with whom there is no variation or shadow of turning." Hebrews 6:13–18 even indicates that God swears by Himself in giving the promise to Abraham and that the surety of this promise is based on the fact that He is unchangeable (Heb. 6:18, Greek, ἀμεταθέτων). This clearly indicates that immutability signifies more than simply God's covenant faithfulness since the assurance of His covenant faithfulness is itself staked on His unchangeable being.[17] If

---

15. Wilhelmus à Brakel explains that in making conditional promises and threats God has not opened Himself up to being moved or determined by the creature. This is because God eternally ordains the relationship between conditionals as well as their fulfillment or nonfulfillment: "He has decreed the cohesive relationship between these matters to be such that it will be well with the righteous and ill with the wicked. If someone improves, repents, and believes, it is the work of God.... God's decree relative to all this is absolute and unconditional: to bring the elect to salvation in the way of repentance and faith, and to damn all others in consequence of their sins." *The Christian's Reasonable Service*, ed. Joel R. Beeke, trans. Bartel Elshout (Grand Rapids: Reformation Heritage Books, 1992), 1:201.

16. à Brakel, *Christian's Reasonable Service*, 1:90.

17. In Genesis 22:16, God says to Abraham, "By Myself I have sworn" (cf. Num. 14:21, 28). This appears to be a reference to the event recorded in Genesis 15:17 in which God symbolically invokes the covenantal curse on His own life by passing between the pieces of severed animals in the theophanic form of a smoking oven and burning torch.

faithfulness itself should be that which constitutes God's immutability, then why offer an oath staked on His own self/life in order to strengthen the assurance that His promise will remain constant? The plain sense appears to be that God's unwavering covenant faithfulness is worthy of our hope precisely because it is rooted in His unwavering and unchangeable being. One reason that change in God, no matter how small, is theologically devastating is that it would signify some alteration in His being or life and thus, to the extent that such change occur, destabilize human confidence in His covenant promises.

Gilles Emery spotlights precisely what is at stake when one accepts mutability in God, observing that "a change requires the acquisition of something new, the introducing of something that was not there before." He continues, "To deny immutability signifies that God acts or finds himself in movement in order to acquire something he was previously lacking, and this would shatter the plentitude and perfection of being that pertains to him."[18] Charnock writes similarly, "If God doth change it must be either to a greater perfection than he had before, or to a less.... If to the better, he was not perfect, and so was not God; if to the worse, he will not be perfect, and so be no longer God after that change."[19] Such is the standard reasoning of classical theism with respect to God's immutability.[20]

Nonliteral Interpretation of Scripture's Mutabilist Language
But what is the classical theist to make of Scripture's prolific use of mutabilist language in referring to God? According to Herman

18. Gilles Emery, "The Immutability of the God of Love and the Problem of Language Concerning the 'Suffering of God,'" in *Divine Impassibility and the Mystery of Human Suffering*, ed. James F. Keating and Thomas Joseph White (Grand Rapids: Eerdmans, 2009), 61.

19. Charnock, *Existence and Attributes*, 1:331.

20. For an insightful treatment of immutability from a classical perspective, see Michael J. Dodds, *The Unchanging God of Love: Thomas Aquinas and Contemporary Theology on Divine Immutability*, 2nd ed. (Washington, D.C.: Catholic University of America Press, 2008). For helpful studies on divine impassibility, see Thomas G. Weinandy, *Does God Suffer?* (Notre Dame, Ind.: University of Notre Dame Press, 2000); and Ronald S. Baines et al., eds., *Confessing the Impassible God: The Biblical, Classical, and Confessional Doctrine of Divine Impassibility* (Palmdale, Calif.: RBAP, 2015).

Bavinck, "Scripture does not contain a few scattered anthropomorphisms but is anthropomorphic through and through."[21] Adherents to the strong account of immutability generally understand the biblical depictions of change in God to be figurative and accommodated expressions designed to convey something true about God, though not under a form of modality proper to Him. The motive for such an interpretation is in many respects the same as the motive for denying that God is really possessed of physical body parts, even though Scripture quite freely attributes bodily features and functions to Him—namely, that nothing denoting finitude, limitation, dependence, or incompleteness of being can be properly said of God. This holds not only with respect to physicalist descriptions of God, but also with respect to any finite and imperfect *modality* that may be ascribed to Him such as that of movement from passive potency to actuality, of becoming and change.

Those who subscribe to the softer version of theistic mutualism are usually willing to deny that the Bible speaks literally or properly of God when it speaks of Him possessing body parts (e.g., Ps. 18:7–9; 89:13; Isa. 65:5), moving about locomotively in space (e.g., Gen. 11:5; Ex. 3:8), or even changing His mind (e.g., Ex. 32:14). But when the Bible speaks of God as experiencing changes of relation, affection, or agency,[22] we are told that these changes are properly in God and that the text would be meaningless or even untrue if this were not so. But it is not at all obvious that this is the case. The classical theist simply regards these as yet further instances of the Bible's anthropomorphic (or anthropopathic) language, revealing something true about God— such as His true opposition to sin, His gracious compassion, or His providential guidance of historical affairs—progressively in time and under a modality (viz., change) that is improper to His plentitude of being. Such improper or nonliteral forms of attribution do not obscure the truth about God any more than talk about God's right arm or

---

21. Bavinck, *Reformed Dogmatics*, 2:99.

22. See, for example, Genesis 6:6; Exodus 22:24; 32:11; Judges 13:25; 1 Samuel 15:11; Isaiah 12:1; 43:24; 44:22; 63:9–10; Ephesians 4:30; and Philippians 1:6. These passages are but a small sample of biblical portrayals of God as changing relationally, emotionally, or in agency of action.

nostrils obscures the truth about Him. Our theology should enable us to discern the various accommodated and nonliteral ways in which God speaks to us about Himself in biblical revelation. Thus, passages depicting God as undergoing change are spoken improperly and from the human vantage point and should not be taken in a strictly literal sense.

God alters the revelation of Himself without altering Himself ontologically. He unchangingly wills changes in His *ad extra* dealings with creatures without willing or experiencing a corresponding change of agency in His own intrinsic actuality. The proper locus of all change is in the revelation of God—as it appears to us successively through various phenomenal instruments—and in the effects of His sovereign administration. Its proper locus is not *in Him* as revealer and administrator. "When repentance is attributed to God," à Brakel writes, "this does not suggest a change in God Himself, but rather a change in activity (in comparison to a prior moment) towards the objects of that activity, this change being according to His immutable decree."[23] It is by rejecting or ignoring the revelation of God's aseity, pure actuality, immutability, simplicity, and so forth that one goes wrong in interpreting the Bible's portrayals of change in God as indicating real changes in His being.

Theistic Mutualism and the Loss of Divine Immutability

Upon considering classical theism's doctrines of divine aseity, pure actuality, and immutability, many modern Calvinist theologians have become convinced that in the historic strong forms of such doctrines other important aspects of God's being are diminished—most notably His interaction with the world. Consider, for instance, the words of Donald Macleod in contrast to those of Calvin, Owen, and à Brakel cited above:

> As things are now, *God's blessedness derives to some extent from his creation.* For example, his profound satisfaction with the work of the six days is registered in the fact that he pronounced it very good (Genesis 1:31), and rested. He expressed similar delight in

---

23. à Brakel, *Christian's Reasonable Service*, 1:101.

the work of the Mediator: "You are my Son, whom I love; with you I am well pleased" (Mark 1:11). And when he presents us to himself "faultless," he does so with great joy (Jude 24).[24]

If God cannot be moved in any way, as the classical position clearly requires, then how can He genuinely relate to us, care for us, and delight in us? How can we have an authentic, personal relationship with Him, and He with us, if there is no give-and-take? Reciprocity and self-giving are the keys to all significant relationships, are they not? If God only gives to us but does not receive from us, then He seems to be missing out on a crucial component of the relationship. This also would seem to cheapen those offerings of worship and service we give to Him, perhaps like giving a present to someone only to discover that it is already possessed; there would be no real need for it. These are not trivial concerns, and they serve as powerful motivation to many who would endeavor to soften the perceived austerity of classical Christian theism.

Such concerns lie at the heart of Isaak Dorner's nineteenth-century revisionist account of God's immutability. He asks, "Does not the living communion of God with the world require divine mutability in some sense? Are not those who stand firm by the concept of an unqualified absolute divine immutability in conflict with the fundamental interests of Christian piety? Don't they lapse into a static and wooden relationship between God and world?"[25] Dorner insists that if God is to genuinely relate Himself to the world of humans in love there must take place "on his side change, alteration, a permitting of himself to be determined."[26]

The burning question seems to be, does the world really matter to God? It is unimaginable that any Christian would want to answer this question in the negative. Yet how does one explain God's care for the world and the nature of His relationship to it? This is the challenge. Does He care for the world in such a way that He allows or ordains creatures to move Him, which would be to allow Himself to be changed

---

24. Donald Macleod, *Shared Life: The Trinity and the Fellowship of God's People* (Fearn, Ross-shire: Christian Focus, 1994), 54. Emphasis mine.

25. Dorner, *Divine Immutability*, 81.

26. Dorner, *Divine Immutability*, 165.

in some way (since all movement is change)? Do creatures contribute to God's being or blessedness? Perhaps these questions are nowhere more acutely felt than with respect to the question of divine impassibility.

By the middle of the twentieth century, it began to be increasingly acceptable within Calvinist circles to challenge the classical doctrine of immutability with regard to God's relationship to the world. Few went so far as to deny the exhaustive foreknowledge and sovereignty of God, but many began to insist that God's relation to the world must consist in an experience He undergoes and in which He is made to feel certain affections vis-à-vis His interaction with creatures. The Presbyterian scholar J. Oliver Buswell, for instance, maintains that "the love of God as represented throughout the Scriptures is totally denied if it does not imply specific chronological relationships between God and His creatures."[27] Buswell believes that if God should not experience change over time in His "intimate actual relationships with His people," then God's love would be reduced "to the frozen wastes of pure speculative abstraction."[28] It seems quite clear that by "intimate actual relationships" Buswell means mutual relationships involving change.

Ronald H. Nash moves in the same direction as Buswell when he concludes, following the lead of the progressive Jesuit scholar W. Norris Clarke, that classical theism can be reconciled to the process theist's demand for a God "who is really related to and thus affected by the creatures who worship him."[29] Nash regards God as subject to change in His relationships with humans. "The Christian theist," he states, "can recognize senses in which even an immutable and perfect God can change. Human beings can make a difference to God."[30]

More recently, D. A. Carson has advanced a similar viewpoint, remarking that "even the most superficial reading of Scripture discloses

27. J. Oliver Buswell, *A Systematic Theology of the Christian Religion* (Grand Rapids: Zondervan, 1962), 1:55. Compare this with Dorner's sentiments: "So also the true *concept of worship* can only emerge from the stated conception of the relation of God to time, from the assumption of an actually historical life of God." *Divine Immutability*, 193.

28. Buswell, *Systematic Theology*, 1:57, 56.

29. Ronald H. Nash, *The Concept of God: An Exploration of Contemporary Difficulties with the Attributes of God* (Grand Rapids: Zondervan, 1983), 99.

30. Nash, *Concept of God*, 105.

God to be a personal Being who interacts with us."[31] In particular, this personal interaction means that God's love for the world is "a vulnerable love that feels pain."[32] For Carson, God's being personal entails that God's relation with the world is mutualistic and genuinely give-and-take. God, he believes, acts on and in the world and is in turn acted upon and moved by His creatures.

Perhaps no recent Calvinist theologian has more steadfastly articulated the demand for an alteration in the conception of divine immutability than Bruce A. Ware. Ware insists upon God's ontological unchangeableness in rather traditional terms, maintaining the "intrinsic immutability of God's own nature." Yet he also contends that God's involvement with creation "includes innumerable changes both on the part of God and on the part of his creatures."[33] Ware calls this "relational mutability."[34] By this term he means that God relates to creatures by virtue of some new state of being He assumes—namely, the new relation—which is something that exists in Him but is really distinct from His nature. This is especially clear in Ware's remarks on God's alleged dispositions: "He changes from anger to mercy, from blessing to cursing, from rejection to acceptance. Each of these changes is real in God, though no such change affects in the slightest the unchangeable supremacy of his intrinsic nature."[35] Ware clearly accepts that two different realities exist in God simultaneously—the one natural (His

---

31. D. A. Carson, *The Difficult Doctrine of the Love of God* (Wheaton, Ill.: Crossway, 2000), 55.

32. Carson, *Difficult Doctrine of the Love of God*, 59.

33. Bruce A. Ware, "An Evangelical Reformulation of the Doctrine of the Immutability of God," *Journal of the Evangelical Theological Society* 29 (December 1986): 433, 438. This article is a distillation of core claims from Ware's 1984 doctoral dissertation at Fuller Theological Seminary, "An Evangelical Reexamination of the Doctrine of the Immutability of God."

34. Ware, "Evangelical Reformulation," 438.

35. Ware, "Evangelical Reformulation," 440–41. Admittedly, it is difficult to square Ware's relational mutability doctrine, which clearly allows affective states of being in God which come and go, with some of his rather strong affirmations of immutability. Consider the following: "Just as it is unthinkable from a biblical point of view that God could ever not be, so too it is unimaginable that God could ever receive some quality, some value, some knowledge, some power, some ability, some perfection that he previously lacked." Bruce A. Ware, *God's Greater Glory: The Exalted God of Scripture and the*

nature or essence) and the other acquired. The older metaphysically-minded theologians might have accurately described this distinction Ware makes as a real distinction between substance (i.e., substantial form or nature) and accidents. According to Ware, some realities in God are identical with His divine nature, and some are not. Those not identical with His divine nature are accidents. It is in the realm of accidental being that Ware locates the changes in God.

The mutualist motivation for Ware's reformulation of divine immutability is made evident in his volume *God's Lesser Glory*. He writes:

> Divine immutability is best understood as involving God's unchangeable nature (ontological immutability) and promise (ethical immutability), but... Scripture does not lead us to think of God as unchangeable in every respect (absolute immutability). Importantly God is changeable *in relationship* with his creation, particularly with human and angelic moral creatures he has made to live in relationship with him. In this relational mutability, God does not change in his essential nature, purpose, will, knowledge, or wisdom; but he does interact with his people in the experiences of their lives as these unfold in time. God actually enters into relationship with his people, while knowing from eternity all that they will face.[36]

A couple objections may be registered in connection to Ware's claims. First, it is incoherent to say that God is ontologically immutable while denying that He is absolutely immutable, unless one believes there are changes in God that are not alterations of actuality or being (which is de facto ontological). But then these changes would not be the alteration of anything real, and therefore any cogent intelligibility of Ware's point collapses. If the mutable relations do really exist in God, as Ware clearly intends, then it turns out that there is in fact ontological mutability in God. This is because relational and accidental states of being are no less ontological—that is, existentially

---

Christian Faith (Wheaton, Ill.: Crossway, 2004), 48. But what are the alleged changing intrinsic states of anger and mercy if not changes of "some quality" of being in God?

36. Bruce A. Ware, *God's Lesser Glory: The Diminished God of Open Theism* (Wheaton, Ill.: Crossway, 2000), 73.

actual—than one's nature or essence. Every state of being, whether essential or nonessential, is an ontological state. Ware appears rather unclear, perhaps even confused, as to the precise meaning and significance of the term "ontological."[37]

Second, when Ware says that God "actually enters into relationship with his people," he means that God is somehow moving along with them in a correlative sense in which He has voluntarily opened Himself up to being affected (i.e., acted upon) and thus changed by the creature. Even if God happens to be the one willing and controlling all of these relational changes, it is still an ontological openness in God to some further determination of (accidental) being for which Ware is arguing, though he may not be fully self-conscious of having embraced ontological mutability. Insisting that these changes in God do not affect God's nature seems irrelevant. No change that has ever touched a creature has produced a real change in its nature either—in its matter or in its being as a particular creaturely suppositum, yes; but in its nature as such, no.[38]

---

37. The modern evangelical muddle with respect to the meaning of the term "being" and its cognates certainly does not begin with Ware. Dorner, for instance, was making similarly confusing statements in the middle of the nineteenth century: "God, in order to be immutable but living love, determines himself to enter into alteration and change, not in respect to his being, but in respect to the exercise of his constantly self-identical love." *Divine Immutability*, 182.

38. It is not uncommon for theistic mutualists desiring to uphold God's immutability to maintain that for all the changes in God, He is still unchanging in His essence or nature. Those who make this claim undoubtedly believe they are saying something important about God. But in truth this fails to say anything particularly unique about God's nature or about the character of His immutability. And the reason is because the same thing could also be said about creatures—that their natures remain unchanged even as they undergo all sorts of nonessential changes. A friend once illustrated this to me by observing that there never was or will be James Dolezal the giraffe. My nature, that feature of my being by virtue of which I am a human and not something else, has never undergone a change and never will (assuming that absolute *exnihilation* and *annihilation* are not properly regarded as changes since nothing persists through such events). But this does not make me immutable. Suffice it to say that affirming God's nature is not altered by other alleged alterations in Him says nothing that could not equally be said of any creature. Both God and the creature are mutable so long as each is susceptible to the acquisition and loss of accidental forms. Affirming constancy in God's nature simply says too little. To truly uphold divine immutability more must be said or

Again, the driving conviction seems to be that anything less than correlative relationality would not count as meaningful interaction between God and His moral creatures. This is the heart of theistic mutualism, and it motivates a key part of Ware's appeal to his open theist counterparts. In fact, he professes a common cause with open theists on precisely this point:

> Open theists are certainly right to seek to ground and embrace the *real relationship* between God and his human creatures, particularly his own people. Classical theism is vulnerable at this point and is in need of some correctives. However, the classical model *can* be modified and *can* sustain the real, vibrant, and reciprocal relationship between God and others. What simply is wrong is the notion that, to uphold the real relatedness of God with others, one must adopt some newer version of freewill theism.[39]

It is crucial to understand that Ware's dispute here is an in-house disagreement with his fellow theistic mutualists. He shares common ground with process and open theists on the question of being and becoming in God. Like them, he endorses the idea of a God who is subject to alterations of being—thus, for Ware, God is becoming in some respect. But in conceding that God is moved by His creatures, Ware does not accept the open theist claim that intelligent creatures are sometimes the independent, autonomous, and original source of change in God. Freewill theism, which Ware rejects, offers a different explanation regarding the *source* of ontological change in God. This

---

assumed about God—for example, that there is nothing in God that is not just His divine essence (i.e., divinity). In that case, all affirmations of God's unchanging nature would be avowals of His absolute immutability. Of course, if all that is in God is just His divine nature, there could be no nonessential actuality in God, and the entire theistic mutualist outlook would fold. This point will be explored further in the discussion about God's simplicity in chapters 3 and 4.

39. Ware, *God's Lesser Glory*, 164. Ware has further advanced his relational mutability doctrine in *God's Greater Glory*, 142–43. He also signals his basic agreement with the process theist Charles Hartshorne on this point, writing, "I think Hartshorne is right…to speak of ways in which God may legitimately be thought of as changeable." "An Exposition and Critique of the Process Doctrines of Divine Mutability and Immutability," *Westminster Theological Journal* 47 (1985): 196.

is where the quarrel lies for Ware. He is concerned with the author ultimately responsible for the changes in God, not whether or not God undergoes change.

The trouble is in seeing how Ware's reciprocally related God bears much resemblance (beyond His power of predestination and fore-knowledge) to the God whom classical theism confesses. Ware surely understates his departure from the classical tradition when he writes, "Obviously some reformulation of classical theism is involved here, but the end product is really only a variation and refinement of the clas-sical model."[40] In truth, the end product is a God who is strikingly *unlike* the God confessed in the classical model. Consider that Ware's account either implicitly or explicitly renders God (1) mutable in being (He begins to be what He was not by acquisition of real, new relations in Himself); (2) passible (moved to new states of affective actuality or being); (3) composed of parts (namely, nature plus newly acquired actualities of relation—to wit, accidents); (4) finite (inasmuch as the changes of relation are said to be *in God* and must bring to Him actu-ality of being He previously lacked); (5) temporally bound (inasmuch as His intrinsic relational mutability necessarily renders Him sub-ject to the measurement of movement, thus locating His existence in time); and (6) certainly not most absolute (as He is made to be actual by virtue of those states of relationality that He acquires from His creatures and which are not strictly identical to His divine essence). It seems more accurate to characterize Ware's theology proper as a form of modified theistic mutualism rather than of modified classical the-ism. I point out Ware's departures from classical Christian theism not to single him out as uniquely progressive or daring, but because his views seem to represent a standard case of what is now perhaps the prevailing outlook among evangelical and Calvinist theologians.

The Sovereignty Solution?
One might wonder how allowing a measure of mutability in God would not undermine His absoluteness and render Him susceptible

---

40. Ware, *God's Lesser Glory*, 164.

to the power of His creatures. Calvinistic theistic mutualists tend to provide the answer that, although God can undergo relational and emotive changes, He only undergoes those changes that He has so willed for Himself. Insofar as the strength of divine immutability has been dialed down to accommodate mutual interaction with the world, the potential vacuum has been filled by dialing up the strength and scope of God's sovereign will.[41] Though God does indeed experience change in Himself, Calvinistic theistic mutualists assure us that all is well since God is in control of those changes. This is what primarily distinguishes their version of theistic mutualism from that of open and process theism.

There are a number of twentieth-century theologians who are precursors to this concept of self-controlled change in God. Karl Barth spoke of a "holy mutability" in God that was subsumed under His lordship. God, he said, partakes in the alterations that creatures undergo. There is also, according to Barth, something that exists in God's essence corresponding to such change.[42] Rather than locate the ultimate authorship of this intrinsic change within the God-head in creatures, which would surely undermine God's freedom and

---

41. For many Calvinistic theistic mutualists, the sovereignty of God is regarded as a central, sufficient dogma. The assumption seems to be that as long as one can continue to maintain God's sovereignty, a number of modifications may legitimately be made to theology proper without jeopardizing one's core Reformed identity. In this vein, Ware maintains that "commitment to a strong and pervasive sovereignty of God…is not by any means all that the Reformed tradition says about God, but it is central to all else that one understands." "A Modified Calvinist Doctrine of God," in *Perspectives on the Doctrine of God: Four Views*, ed. Bruce A. Ware (Nashville: B&H Academic, 2008), 77. I submit that this elevation of the divine will to the status of a controlling, central dogma is itself out of step with classical Reformed orthodoxy's antivoluntarism and its doctrine of divine simplicity. The will of God is not really distinct from any other aspect of God's being and certainly does not exercise causal or determinative power over other features of God's intrinsic actuality.

42. See Karl Barth, *Church Dogmatics* II/1, trans. T. H. L. Parker, et al. (Edinburgh: T&T Clark, 1957), 496 (§31.2). "There is such a thing as a holy mutability in God. He is above all ages. But above them as their Lord [1 Tim. 1:17]…and therefore as One who—as Master and in His own way—partakes in their alteration, so that there is something corresponding to that alteration in His own essence. His constancy consists in the fact that He is always the same in every change."

sovereignty, Barth proposes that God is self-moved: "The personal God has a heart. He can feel and be affected. He is not impassible. He cannot be moved from outside by an extraneous power. But this does not mean that He is not capable of moving Himself. No, God is moved and stirred, yet not like ourselves in powerlessness, but in His own free power, in His innermost being: moved and touched by Himself."[43]

Thomas F. Tracy also anticipates this recent shift toward a mutable God who controls His own development. Tracy's concerns are clearly those of a theistic mutualist:

> Should we say that God is *actus purus* in the scholastic sense, we would not be able to understand his relation to creatures and their history except in his functions as Ultimate Cause, reducing potentiality to actuality in other things without himself undergoing any change. This makes it difficult to do justice, however, to the richness of the relationship between God and humankind that appears in the narrative sources and devotional traditions of Judaism and Christianity. We must not exclude the possibility that God may establish a relation to creatures in which he is genuinely affected by them and yet does not cease to be God.[44]

Tracy stoutly maintains that the power of God's will controls and regulates this openness to being acted upon by creatures. "God's continued existence," he explains, "cannot be dependent upon the actions of any other being *unless he intends that it be*."[45] Thus, God is unchanging unless He sovereignly chooses to change or be changed. We might wonder how such an approach can avoid a doctrine of divine self-creativity, when God wills an actuality of being for Himself that is not

---

43. Barth, *Church Dogmatics* II/1, 370 (§30.2). It bears pointing out that Barth in his statements, unlike many modern evangelicals who follow him, does not say that God freely wills to be moved instrumentally *by creatures*, but only that He freely wills to move Himself. This is sufficient to establish that Barth does not hold the classical immutability doctrine and has instead replaced it with a doctrine of divine self-controlled mutability and passibility. Nevertheless, Barth appears to resist the more radical proposal that God's self-movement includes the choice to be moved by His creatures.

44. Thomas F. Tracy, *God, Action, and Embodiment* (Grand Rapids: Eerdmans, 1984), 129.

45. Tracy, *God, Action, and Embodiment*, 128. Emphasis mine.

identical with His divine essence. And Tracy boldly embraces precisely that implication: "God can be said to be self-creative in the sense that he determines the content of his own existence. God, that is, freely prescribes the pattern of activity that constitutes his life."[46] One obvious consequence is that God is Himself created and caused to be to the extent that He wills alterations in being for Himself.[47] God thus appears to be partly Creator and partly created.

Unfortunately, this notion of divinely controlled change in God's being is not the exclusive domain of Barthian actualists and soft process theists like Tracy. Some modern Calvinistic evangelicals advance almost the same belief. Bruce Ware signals his agreement with Barth's notion of "holy mutability."[48] J. I. Packer walks the same path when he speaks of God experiencing creatures, thus indicating that creatures can act upon God in some respect. Packer goes decidedly further in the direction of theistic mutualism than Barth was willing to go. Packer explains that "God's experiences do not come upon him as ours come upon us, for his are foreknown, willed, and chosen by himself, and are not involuntary surprises forced on him from outside, *apart from his own decision*, in the way that ours regularly are."[49] Packer, like Tracy, means to say that God *is* moved by the creature in His unfolding experiences, though always in accordance with His own will to be

---

46. Tracy, *God, Action, and Embodiment*, 126.

47. Note that an alteration in being does not necessarily mean alteration in essence, as so many nowadays mistakenly presume. A thing's being involves all that it is, including those aspects of it that are not strictly identical with its essence, such as its act of existence (*esse*) and any accidents it may acquire. Of course, in an absolutely simple God, such as is confessed by classical Christian theism, there is no distinction between existence and essence, and there are no accidents.

48. Ware, "Exposition and Critique of the Process Doctrines of Divine Mutability and Immutability," 196n59.

49. J. I. Packer, "Theism for Our Time," in *God Who Is Rich in Mercy*, ed. Peter T. O'Brien and David G. Peterson (Grand Rapids: Baker, 1986), 17. Emphasis mine. As an aside, I find the whole notion that God has "experiences" to be wrongheaded. An experiencer must be acted upon and so receive a determination of being from another. Experience requires that something "happen to" the individual going through the experience. But nothing "happens to" or befalls God since He is pure act. Herbert McCabe is correct when he writes, "Whatever the consciousness of the creator may be, it cannot be that of an experiencer confronted by what he experiences." *God Matters*, 45.

so moved. This insistence on divine self-control is particularly clear when Packer speaks about God's so-called feelings:

> God's feelings are not beyond his control, as ours often are. Theologians express this by saying that God is impassible. They mean not that he is impassive and unfeeling but that what he feels, like what he does, is a matter of his own deliberate, voluntary choice and is included in the unity of his infinite being. God is never our victim in the sense that we make him suffer *where he had not first chosen to suffer*. Scriptures expressing the reality of God's emotions (joy, sorrow, anger, delight, love, hate, etc.) abound, however, and it is a great mistake to forget that God feels—though in a way of necessity that transcends a finite being's experience of emotion.[50]

Packer's point is clearly that God has emotions He acquires by virtue of His choice and in correlation to creaturely actions of which He feels the effects. In this sense, these are states of emotive actuality or being that God possesses in distinction from His essence.[51] Packer's concession that God can choose to suffer (that is, to be acted upon and so receive actuality in some fashion) at the hands of His creatures is where we discover his theistic mutualism and willingness to allow a measure of mutability in God. Again, as long as God freely chooses to permit these changes in Himself, we are assured all is well.

Finally, this notion of self-controlled mutability in God is also advanced by Rob Lister in his volume *God Is Impassible and Impassioned*. He writes, "In the main the classical tradition simply sought to preserve the notion that, as the self-determined sovereign, God is not

---

50. J. I. Packer, *Concise Theology: A Guide to Historic Christian Beliefs* (Carol Stream, Ill.: Tyndale House, 1993), 29. Emphasis mine. It is demonstrably certain that self-controlled, emotive change is not what was historically intended by the doctrine of divine impassibility. Barth seems to have recognized this fact and for that reason denied divine impassibility. It was simply not compatible with his voluntarist notion of God as willing intrinsic changes for Himself. For a fine collection of classical Reformed texts on divine impassibility, see Samuel Renihan, ed., *God without Passions: A Reader* (Palmdale, Ca.: RBAP, 2015).

51. Presumably, Packer does not hold that God's essence or nature is the subject of God's free determining choice.

subject to emotional affects that are *involuntarily* or *unexpectedly* wrung from him by creatures."[52] It is clear that Lister understands that God is subject to self-willed emotive changes that His creatures produce in Him. God may be subject to emotional effects wrung from Him as long as He is the one who sovereignly wills the wringing. This is exactly Tracy's point when he says that God cannot be dependent on the actions of others unless He chooses so to be. This is also Packer's point—God does not suffer action upon Himself from creatures unless He so chooses. Also, it is clear that Lister does not mean that God can variously alter the *manifestation* of Himself toward creatures, as classical Christian theism affirms, but rather that God wills changes that occur in His own being. God's responsiveness to His creatures involves "a transition that occurs *in God*."[53] Lister calls this divine self-control God's "emotional sovereignty" and "sovereign emotional lordship."[54] This is a sovereignty that God exercises over His own intrinsic being, an actuality of being that in part He has freely chosen for Himself and that comes to Him by way of mutualistic interaction with His creatures. This is surely divine self-creativity, as Tracy rightly recognizes.

Again, this notion of God as Lord and Sovereign over His own being and who voluntarily produces changes in Himself (or ordains others to produce them) is calculated to shore up any potential

---

52. Rob Lister, *God Is Impassible and Impassioned: Toward a Theology of Divine Emotion* (Wheaton, Ill.: Crossway, 2012), 33. Lister mistakes the "classical tradition" for holding to some form of voluntarism. His conclusion stems from his unfounded assumption that all traditional denials of creaturely control over God must be because the tradition held God to be voluntarily self-controlled. But for the classical tradition the opposite of creaturely control over God is not divine self-control; rather, it is the pure actuality of God. As purely actual and perfectly simple, God cannot possibly be controlled, either by others or by Himself. Such self-control would necessitate a real distinction in God between that which controls—presumably the divine will—and that which is controlled. Lister almost entirely ignores the role played by pure actuality and simplicity in the classical understanding of God's impassibility.

53. Lister, *God Is Impassible and Impassioned*, 179. Emphasis mine. Lister follows Ware in distinguishing between God's eternal "intrinsic nature" and His temporally acquired relations. Both are said to be "in God." It should be pointed out that this is wholly incongruous with the classical doctrine of divine simplicity. I shall return to this point in chapters 3 and 4.

54. Lister, *God Is Impassible and Impassioned*, 167–68.

liabilities from having first divested God of His absolute immutability. And the motivation for that divestment is nothing other than theistic mutualism, the belief that any meaningful relationship between God and man must involve God in a transaction wherein He receives some determination of being from His creatures.

Conclusion

If one follows the path of theistic mutualism, even if it is modified by the belief that God freely chooses and controls His mutability, then it turns out that a man *can* be profitable to God, a righteous man *can* produce pleasure in Him that He would otherwise be lacking, and it *is* gain to God if we make our ways perfect. Moreover, God *does* receive from us and *is* served by human hands. These outcomes would not be any less real if God should simply choose to place Himself in this position of being acted upon by His creatures. This modified account of divine immutability with its attendant notion of a God who freely chooses aspects of His own intrinsic being seems to be on a collision course with the classical doctrines of divine aseity and immutability.[55] Indeed, it must mean that God Himself lives, moves, and has His being (i.e., His actuality) in or through His creatures in some respect. The advocates of this position tell us that He has chosen this for Himself. In opposition, the traditional notion of divine aseity is captured well when Arthur W. Pink states that God "gives to all and is enriched by none."[56] This can no longer be said by those Calvinists who have fallen under the spell of theistic mutualism. Rather, they must concede that God gives to all and in turn freely chooses to be enriched by some of His creatures.

Pressing the implications of this new trajectory a bit further, we must ask: If God should be able to will a measure of mutability for Himself, then what other of His attributes, if any, would He be permitted to augment or negate? Eternity? Simplicity? Infinity?

---

55. Steven Duby observes that "only a substantially modified (and perhaps incoherent) version of aseity can claim that God is uncaused and chooses to be causally affected by his creatures." *Divine Simplicity*, 195.

56. Arthur W. Pink, *Gleanings in the Godhead* (Chicago: Moody, 1975), 13.

Invisibility? Immortality? Omniscience? Omnipotence? Omnipresence? In truth, a number of these other divine attributes have already been "reformulated"—or, more accurately, abandoned—such as impassibility, timeless eternity, and simplicity. And what about the so-called moral attributes such as love, mercy, justice, and truth? Can these be voluntarily suspended in order to make God's relationship to us more "personal" and genuinely reciprocal? Theistic mutualism, when consistently developed, is like an acid that cannot but burn through a whole host of divine attributes traditionally confessed of God. When its work is done, the result looks rather unlike a variation or refinement of the classical model and much more like a demolition and wholesale replacement.[57]

---

57. What makes this demolition and replacement difficult to detect, perhaps, is that the replacement model for classical Christian theism insists on retaining the idioms and language of the old theological structure it has torn down. In fact, some of those who have pulled apart the older orthodoxy seem genuinely unaware of having done so. And, furthermore, many of those theistic mutualists who have been undermining the classical doctrine of God have produced sound and traditionally-minded scholarship in other areas of doctrine. All these factors make it challenging to place a strong injunction against their innovative teachings on theology proper.

CHAPTER 3

Simple God

Throughout the course of church history, theologians have sought to coherently communicate both the explicit teachings of Scripture and the doctrines that emerge as a necessary consequence of what the Bible as a whole teaches. These truths rightly ordered form an internally consistent system of Christian doctrine. We might liken the work of the theologian to that of a builder, who first gathers materials for the construction of a building and then proceeds to erect the structure. Some of the materials are easily collected, while others are obtained with much difficulty. But the work is not finished when one has gathered the various resources. There remains the difficult job of arranging them in their proper order so that the building holds itself together. The task of theology proper is similar. After gathering the various truths about God that are spread throughout nature and Scripture, one is faced with the challenge of intelligibly arranging the doctrines so as to form a single coherent doctrine of God.

Of course there must be rules to govern this task, just as there are blueprints governing the construction of a building. Otherwise, the project proceeds without rhyme or reason, and certain parts may be at odds with other parts, compromising the integrity of the whole. Paul Helm observes that classical Christian theism has offered just such a set of rules, a "grammatical template," by which we are enabled to coherently hold together the diversity of biblical statements about God. He explains:

> The data regarding the essence and nature of God, as revealed
> in Scripture, have by and large an occasional and unsystematic

character to them. But because Scripture, as God's word, is self-consistent, the varied data must be self-consistent, and when properly appreciated must also be *seen* to be. Or, at the very least, it may be recognized that alleged inconsistency cannot be proven. The classical conceptual shape of Christian theism offers a template in terms of which that consistency may be appreciated. For it provides rules, drawn from the varied data of Scripture, in terms of which the varied language of Scripture about God, not only in his unity but also in his trinitarian glory and his actions in the economy of redemption, can be learned and used without falling into inconsistency or serious error. It is not so much an explanatory as a *grammatical template*.[1]

This grammar establishes an acceptable framework for our God-talk and sets certain controls on what theological proposals we should and should not regard as sound. The goal is not to enable us to comprehend God in some scientific sense or to dispel the mystery of His being. Indeed, classical Christian theism insists upon the absolute incomprehensibility of God throughout its entire formulation. The Puritan Stephen Charnock offers sage counsel when he states, "Though we cannot comprehend him as he is, we must be careful not to fancy him to be what he is not."[2] The Swiss theologian Charles Journet proposes that "the aim of the theologian dealing with a mystery is to do away with phrases which diminish the mystery."[3] Our theological grammar functions in part to preserve the integrity of the revealed mystery of God at precisely those points where human reason may be tempted to diminish it in an effort to render God more easily understood by the human intellect.

This brings us to the doctrine of divine simplicity. Throughout most of church history, divine simplicity served as the indispensable centerpiece in the "grammar" regulating theology proper. It was presumed as

---

1. Paul Helm, foreword to James E. Dolezal, *God without Parts: Divine Simplicity and the Metaphysics of God's Absoluteness* (Eugene, Ore.: Pickwick Publications, 2011), ix.

2. Charnock, *Existence and Attributes*, 1:197.

3. Charles Journet, *The Meaning of Evil*, trans. Michael Barry (New York: P. J. Kennedy and Sons, 1963), 14.

a baseline that none dared transgress. The doctrine's refinement and clarification reached its apex in the medieval period, but this height of development was by no means the beginning of its demise. Simplicity continued to be confessed and defended by the vast majority of Catholics and Protestants alike well into the second century of the Protestant Reformation era. Anglicans, Presbyterians, Congregationalists, and Baptists all confessed that God is "without parts." The Belgic Confession even made divine simplicity its opening affirmation: "We all believe with the heart, and confess with the mouth, that there is one only simple and spiritual Being, which we call God."[4] The Anglican scholar Peter Sanlon has recently stressed the primacy of this doctrine, declaring, "The simplicity of God is the most fundamental doctrinal grammar of divinity."[5]

Yet divine simplicity is either entirely missing or severely underappreciated in the writings of evangelical theistic mutualists. This has played no small part in the progressive disintegration of classical Christian theism among evangelicals. Many who bother to mention divine simplicity at all tend to disparage it as a philosophical relic that the church is wise to disregard. This trend is not particularly new. In the early part of the twentieth century, Louis Berkhof observed, "In recent works on theology the simplicity of God is seldom mentioned. Many theologians positively deny it, either because it is regarded as a purely metaphysical abstraction, or because, in their estimation, it conflicts with the doctrine of the Trinity."[6] The Catholic author

---

4. Belgic Confession, article 1 (1561), in James T. Dennison, *Reformed Confessions of the 16th and 17th Centuries in English Translation* (Grand Rapids: Reformation Heritage Books, 2008–2014), 2:425. See also the Thirty-Nine Articles, article 1 (1563); Westminster Confession of Faith 2.1 (1647); Savoy Declaration 2.1 (1658); and the Second London Confession of Faith 2.1 (1677/1689).

5. Peter Sanlon, *Simply God: Recovering the Classical Trinity* (Nottingham, England: Inter-Varsity, 2014), 58.

6. Louis Berkhof, *Systematic Theology* (Grand Rapids: Eerdmans, 1996), 62. More recently, there seems to have been a slight uptick in support for divine simplicity, or for some modified form of it. See the work of the following evangelicals: Millard J. Erickson, *God the Father Almighty: A Contemporary Exploration of the Divine Attributes* (Grand Rapids: Baker, 1998), 210–32; Wayne Grudem, *Systematic Theology: An Introduction to Biblical Doctrine* (Grand Rapids: Zondervan, 1994), 177–80; K. Scott

F. J. Sheed, writing around the same time as Berkhof, offers a similarly sobering assessment: "A study of what is happening to theology in its higher reaches would almost certainly take as its starting point the attribute of simplicity, and show that every current heresy begins by being wrong on that."[7]

For most Christians, even for those whose ecclesiastical confessions contain the doctrine, divine simplicity is perhaps completely unheard of. It may even sound strange to say that God is simple. We are inclined to say the opposite: God is complex! So what is this teaching, and why is it so important to our doctrine of God? I will first set forth the basic claims and implications of the doctrine of divine simplicity. Second, I will identify the biblical motivations underlying it. Finally, the historical witness to the doctrine will be briefly considered. My purpose in this chapter is primarily to reintroduce this fundamental piece of classical Christian orthodoxy. In chapter 4, I will examine some of the ways in which evangelical theistic mutualists fall foul of this teaching.

Basic Claims and Implications of Divine Simplicity

The principal claim of divine simplicity is that God is not composed of parts. Whatever is composed of parts depends upon its parts in order to be as it is. A part is anything in a subject that is less than the whole and without which the subject would be really different than it is. In short, composite beings need their parts in order to exist as they do. Moreover, the parts in an integrated whole require a composer distinct from themselves to unify them, an extrinsic source of unity. If God should be composed of parts—of components that were prior to Him in being—He would be doubly dependent: first, on the parts, and second, on the composer of the parts.[8] But God is absolute in being, alone

---

Oliphint, God with Us: Divine Condescension and the Attributes of God (Wheaton, Ill.: Crossway, 2012), 17–18, 63–67.

7. F. J. Sheed, "The Modern Attitude to God," in C. Lattey, ed., God: Papers Read at the Summer School of Catholic Studies, Held at Cambridge, July 26th—August 4th, 1930 (London: Sheed and Ward, 1931), 232.

8. "Composition is the essential mark of being constituted by principles or causes, in the light of which the composed thing becomes intelligible. What is composed is thus

the sufficient reason for Himself and all other things, and so cannot in any respect derive His being from another. Because God cannot depend on what is not God in order to be God, theologians traditionally insist that all that is in God is God.[9]

A number of implications follow from this basic conviction. First, God's existence (act of being) and essence (quiddity) cannot be constituent components in Him, each supplying what the other lacks. Rather, God must be identical with His existence and essence, and they must be identical with each other. It is His essence to be. Strictly speaking, His act of existence is not what He *has*, but what He *is*.[10] Similarly, God does not merely instantiate divinity as a particular concrete instance of it. Rather, He is divinity itself. No man is humanity as such, but God is divinity as such. Many theologians even conclude

---

necessarily derivative in character, and as such dependent upon something that is simple and prior." Rudi A. te Velde, *Aquinas on God: The "Divine Science" of the* Summa Theologiae (Aldershot, U.K.: Ashgate, 2006), 78. The dependency of composite beings upon that which is simple and prior denotes dependency in the absolute sense rather than the relative. After all, within the creaturely order composite beings frequently bring forth other composite beings that depend upon them in some respect.

9. Consider the words of the medieval theologian Thomas Aquinas: "Every composite is posterior to its components: since the simpler exists in itself before anything is added to it for the composition of a third. But nothing is prior to the first. Therefore, since God is the first principle, He is not composite." *Scriptum super libros Sententiarum*, I.8.4.1, in *Thomas Aquinas's Earliest Treatment of the Divine Essence*: Scriptum super libros Sententiarum, Book I, Distinction 8, trans. E. M. Macierowski (Binghamton, N.Y.: Binghamton University, 1998). Charnock writes similarly, "God is the most simple being; for that which is first in nature, having nothing beyond it, cannot by any means be thought to be compounded; for whatsoever is so, depends upon the parts whereof it is compounded, and so is not the first being: now God being infinitely simple, *hath nothing in himself which is not himself*, and therefore cannot will any change in himself, he being his own essence and existence." *Existence and Attributes*, 1:333. Emphasis mine.

10. Perhaps in order to appreciate the force of this one should consider that in every creature existence and essence must be really distinct principles of being. Existence is that by which a things *is*; essence is that by which is it is *what* it is. Louis De Raeymaeker explains, "À propos of every being two questions are raised: 'Is it?' and 'What is it?' These questions are as irreducible as their answers. To one who asks what is man we do not answer by saying that men actually exist; and to one who asks if men exist it is not at all opportune to answer that man is a rational animal. This adequate opposition ought to make us conclude to a real distinction." *The Philosophy of Being*, trans. Edmund H. Ziegelmeyer (St. Louis: B. Herder, 1954), 102–3.

that God's essential identity with His own existence is the ontological foundation of His name "I AM" (Ex. 3:14).

Second, if all that is in God is God, then each of His attributes is identical with His essence. By contrast, most of a creature's attributes are not identical with its essence. A man or woman may be good, wise, just, merciful, and the like. But these are not identical with their human essence. Consider the many humans who do not exhibit any of these attributes and yet are possessed of the same human essence. Thus, in humans these attributes are realities that add some quality of being in addition to the substantial form of humanity. But if God is simple, there can be no real distinction between His essence (or substantial form) and attributes. The Puritan George Swinnock, in discussing the meaning of simplicity, asserts, "God is all essence, all being, and nothing else."[11] God does not depend on qualities really distinct from His divine essence in order to exist as He does. He does not require what is not God (i.e., not divinity) in order to be anything that He is.

It further follows from God's non-compositeness that in Him all His attributes are really identical with each other. For many, this implication is the hardest to accept. It would seem that if we know anything about God, then we know that His power is not His wisdom, and His wisdom is not His goodness, and His goodness is not His eternity, and so on. But if He is simple, and if His being is not dependent on component parts that are ontologically more basic than the fullness of His being, then all these things we say about Him would have to be identical in Him. The Puritan John Owen thus concludes, "*The attributes of God*, which alone seem to be distinct things in the essence of God, *are all of them essentially the same with one another*, and every one the same with the essence of God itself."[12] Swinnock likewise asserts that God's attributes "are one indivisible essence, to will and to understand, and to love and to hate, and to be, *are all the same and one in God*."[13]

---

11. George Swinnock, *The Incomparableness of God*, in *The Works of George Swinnock* (1868; repr., Edinburgh: Banner of Truth Trust, 1992), 4:397.

12. John Owen, *Vindicae Evangelicae*, in *The Works of John Owen*, ed. William Goold (1850–1853; repr., Edinburgh: Banner of Truth Trust), 12:72.

13. Swinnock, *Incomparableness of God*, in *Works*, 4:397. Emphasis mine.

God's essence is not simply a bundle of contiguous properties or attributes, each existing alongside the others as an integrated whole. His divinity is not a sublime set of great-making properties all splendidly arranged together in Him. In His essence, it is not one thing to be good, another to be wise, another to be powerful, and so on. Rather, the reality in virtue of which all these things are truly said of God is nothing but His own simple divinity. Properly speaking, God is good by virtue of God, not goodness. He is wise by virtue of God, not wisdom. He is powerful by virtue of God, not power. He is love by virtue of God, not love. And when we say that God is goodness itself, wisdom itself, power itself, and love itself, we do not mean that these are so many really distinct parts or forms in God, but simply that He is all that is involved in these terms by virtue of His own divine essence as such.[14] God is not the particular instantiation of a wonderful *set* of properties. Rather, there is nothing in God that is not identical with His divinity, nothing that is not just God Himself.

---

14. In light of the strong identity claims of the classical simplicity doctrine, some wonder what we are to make of the distinctions made among the divine attributes in our God-talk. Does not the real identity of these things in God render meaningless the distinctions we tend to draw among His attributes in our theologizing? In response, it should be observed that the distinctions we make among the attributes in our God-talk follow from the manner in which God's perfection is revealed, not from the manner in which it exists in Him. Inasmuch as the language and imagery by which God reveals Himself in nature and Scripture draw upon a vast range of really distinct perfections in the created order, so likewise human speech about Him tends to follow the same route in the distinctions it makes. Each attribute, in its distinction from all others, enables us to glimpse a sliver of the perfect fullness of God's being. The *manner* in which we know and talk about His perfection does not—indeed, cannot!—correspond univocally to the way God is in Himself. Rather, in revelation He refracts through the prism of creation and history His perfect fullness of simple being. What is simple in Him thus appears to us under the form of a spectrum of distinct virtues. George Hayward Joyce offers useful insight in this regard: "Our minds can form no single concept to express that all-embracing unity of [God's] being: our only resource is to form partial concepts, each of which exhibits some aspect of Divine fullness.... The attributes...are not distinct determinations in God, as are justice and mercy in man: the distinction is the work of the mind. But it is grounded on the reality, because the fullness of the Divine being contains all that is involved in these terms." *Principles of Natural Theology*, 3rd ed. (London: Longmans, Green, 1951), 260–61.

Peter Sanlon is surely correct when he observes that simplicity "makes claims about God that are profound, counter-intuitive, [and] difficult to articulate" and that it "recasts everything we say about God."[15] Yet, for all this, the doctrine's fundamental rationale is compelling. All parts are principles and determinations of being that are really distinct from those entities in which they are incorporated. Those things composed of parts thus depend on sources of being and actuality really distinct from and prior to themselves. *But God cannot depend on what is not Himself in order to be Himself.* God is not the consequence of any actualizing principle more primitive than His own divinity. Whatever else we may say about God, the mysterious truth of His absoluteness must not be compromised or dissipated. Wilhelmus à Brakel counsels that since "all composition implies imperfection, dependency, and divisibility, we must not think of God as being composite even in the remotest sense of the word."[16] If this compels us to make a number of peculiar claims about God, so be it.

Biblical Basis for Divine Simplicity

Having stipulated the basic sense of the doctrine, we must now examine the biblical motives underlying it. Does the Bible really require adherence to divine simplicity?

There is no single biblical proof text for this doctrine. It follows, rather, by way of good and necessary consequence from a number of other doctrines that are clearly taught in Scripture. And though the cognitive realization of divine simplicity requires that we contemplate the implications of other doctrines, it is not for that reason any less biblical.[17] All that is explicitly stated in Scripture and all that must necessarily follow from Scripture must equally be regarded as the Bible's

---

15. Sanlon, *Simply God*, 58.

16. à Brakel, *Christian's Reasonable Service*, 1:96.

17. In claiming that divine simplicity is a biblical doctrine, it does not follow that one can only arrive at this doctrine by considering the biblical witness. As suggested in the remarks of Aquinas and Charnock above, one can also arrive at the conclusion that God is simple by contemplating what is required in order for Him to be the first cause of being. The truth that God is *causa prima* is not exclusively conveyed to us through Holy Scripture. Even so, many things witnessed and entailed in God's disclosure of

teaching. Simplicity, much like the doctrine of the Trinity, makes the best sense of the revealed data on God considered altogether. I will spotlight three biblical doctrines that necessitate the truth of God's simplicity: divine independence, infinity, and creation.

Independence

If God is *a se* (of Himself), then it follows that He does not derive any aspect of Himself—existence, essence, attributes, activity—from another. Negatively, we indicate this by insisting that God is independent in being. We have seen in the previous chapter that He is not served by human hands, as though He needed anything (Acts 17:25). He is the giver of being, not the receiver of it. For this reason, He is in no one's debt. The apostle Paul asks in Romans 11:35, "Who has first given to Him, and it shall be repaid to him?" As no one supplies to God what He lacks, He is indebted to none (cf. Job 35:7–8; 41:11). It would be odd if an affirmation of divine independence applied only to God's relationship with select creatures in certain situations. The sense of these passages is rather that God does not receive anything whatsoever from outside Himself.[18]

Scripture affirms God's independence in a variety of ways. God does not derive knowledge from outside Himself, and neither is He informed by creatures (Isa. 40:14). His will is independent and so is not compelled by any other. As Nebuchadnezzar declared after God humbled him,

> All the inhabitants of the earth are reputed as nothing;
> He does according to His will in the army of heaven
> And among the inhabitants of the earth.
> No one can restrain His hand
> Or say to Him, "What have You done?" (Dan. 4:35).

Himself in nature are also witnessed and entailed in the disclosure of Himself in Scripture.

18. This is not to suggest that God is self-caused or self-derived. Nothing can be properly self-caused since it cannot give itself what it lacks and it cannot receive from itself what it already possesses.

Psalm 115:3 emphasizes the independence of divine power by affirming that God "does whatever He pleases." His love also is independent
of the creature. He says of unlovely and wicked Israel, "I will heal their
backsliding, I will love them freely" (Hos. 14:4). The point is that He
is not *moved* to love sinners by any loveliness that is in them.

Perhaps the most prominent biblical witness to God's independence is the revelation of His divine name, "I AM," in Exodus 3:14. In
the context, God is reassuring Moses and Israel of His all-sufficiency
to accomplish the great work of their redemption from Egypt. He
grounds this perfect covenantal sufficiency on the perfect sufficiency of
His own being, denoted by His name. How can we be absolutely sure
that God's covenantal promises and work on our behalf will not fail?
Only if He is utterly self-sufficient at the level of His very being. By
identifying Himself with His own existence, which is one implication
of His revealed name, God declares that He is wholly independent of
others and thus that our faith in Him need not be ultimately grounded
in some source of reliability that lies outside of or prior to Him. The
dependability of God's ways in redemptive history is rooted in His
history-transcending self-sufficient act of existence.[19]

---

19. Some scholars balk at the idea of suggesting that the revelation of the divine
name in Exodus 3:14 carries any implications for our understanding of divine ontology.
Aidan Nichols offers a reasonable rejoinder to this criticism: "Although a biblical scholarship more attuned to the nuances of the Hebrew original would want to find more
in the revelation of the divine name than simply metaphysics, it is hard to deny that
the biblical author is making some kind of statement about the God of the Fathers as a
unique referent of the language of being. To this extent—a considerable extent!—the
ancient and medieval exegesis of what is on any showing a key text of the biblical revelation is abundantly justified." *Discovering Aquinas: An Introduction to His Life, Work, and
Influence* (Grand Rapids: Eerdmans, 2003), 43. While the revelation of the divine name
to Moses in the context of God's purpose to deliver Israel from their Egyptian bondage
is meant primarily to assure God's people of His perfect covenantal sufficiency, it is not
for that reason not also a revelation of His unique and transcendent manner of being.
In fact, the truth revealed about God's *being* appears to be offered to engender human
confidence in His covenantal and redemptive reliability. Matthew Levering explains
that God's name as "I AM" destroys our conceptual idolatries in which we conceive
of God as something contained in our minds and within the finite order of categorical being: "Knowing God as sheer infinite 'being' does not involve capturing God in a
concept; on the contrary, a proper apprehension of God as 'I am who I am' destroys all
conceptual idolatries that seek to place God *within* a finite creaturely category." *Scripture*

The Second London Confession of Faith 2.1 affirms this doctrine when it states that God's "subsistence is in and of Himself." The confession further elaborates this same truth in 2.2: "God, having all life (John 5:26), glory (Ps. 138:13), goodness (Ps. 119:68), blessedness, in and of Himself, is alone in and unto Himself all-sufficient, not standing in need of any creature which He hath made, nor deriving any glory from them (Job 22:2–3).... His knowledge is infinite, infallible, and independent upon the creature, so as nothing is to Him contingent or uncertain (Ezek. 11:5; Acts 15:18)."[20]

The implications of God's independence for divine simplicity should be clear. If God possesses His existence, essence, or attributes as so many determinations of being—which they would be if they were in Him as distinct parts and constituents—then in fact He is indebted to that which is not God for the fullness of His being. As for our trust in Him, if God is composed of parts—which, as parts, must necessarily be distinct from the fullness of God's being as God—then our confidence in Him must look to some source of being prior to Him, a reality more fundamental than Himself. This is what divine aseity and independence proscribes. Thus, all that is in God must be God.

Infinity
Classic Christian theism maintains that God is in every way infinite. Scripture teaches divine infinity when it speaks of God's greatness as exalted above all creation. God's glory is above the heavens (Ps. 8:1; 148:13), and even the heaven of heavens cannot contain Him (1 Kings 8:27; 2 Chron. 2:6; 6:18). His greatness is unfathomable (Ps. 145:3), and no one can discover the limit of the Almighty (Job 11:7). Other passages that speak of God's infinity include those that attest to His fullness of being. God says to Israel in Isaiah 48:12, "I am He, I am the First, I am also the Last" (cf. 41:4; 44:6). This fullness of being sets Him

---

and *Metaphysics: Aquinas and the Renewal of Trinitarian Theology* (Oxford: Blackwell Publishing, 2004), 67. This is what was needed if Israel was to understand the utter reliability of God.

20. Second London Confession of Faith, in Dennison, *Reformed Confessions*, 4:535–36.

apart from all false gods and indeed all finite beings of any sort. This same truth is conveyed in the parallel expression in Revelation 1:8, "I am the Alpha and the Omega" (cf. 1:11, 17; 2:8; 21:6; 22:13). God is not an alpha who is in progress toward an omega point of being. He does not advance toward an end of being with which He is not eternally identical. He is the fullness of being or, as Herman Bavinck so beautifully puts it, "an immeasurable and unbounded ocean of being."[21]

Touching the question of God's simplicity, whatever is perfectly infinite in being cannot be built up from that which is finite in being. But parts of a thing must necessarily be finite. Every part, insomuch as it is neither identical with the whole nor with other parts, must lack the existence and perfection proper to those things outside itself. And any whole is necessarily greater than its parts in some respects. All forms of composition thus entail that each constituent part or principle be finite.[22] What is more, no set of finite properties, however impressive, could yield an actually infinite being.[23] In order to be genu-

---

21. Bavinck, *Reformed Dogmatics*, 2:123. The entire passage in which that statement appears is worthy of consideration: "God is the real, the true being, the fullness of being, the sum total of all reality and perfection, the totality of being, from which all other being owes its existence. He is an immeasurable and unbounded ocean of being; the absolute being who alone has being in himself. Now, this description of God's being deserves preference over that of personality, love, fatherhood, and so forth, because it encompasses all of God's attributes in an absolute sense. In other words, by this description, God is recognized and confirmed as God in all his perfections."

22. Steven Duby offers helpful insight on this point: "God's infinity implies that he is really identical with each of his attributes and is therefore not composed of substance and accidents. God's essence and attributes are utterly replete with no limit or lack in Holy Scripture so that God is all that he is in a singular plentitude. If the perfections were taken to be multiple actual infinites, these would have to be differentiated from one another so that, in the end, each would lack something in the others and prove to be limited and finite. Therefore, the infinity of God entails that he is not composed of really distinct attributes." *Divine Simplicity*, 157. See also Charnock, *Existence and Attributes*, 1:186.

23. Richard Muller points out that Thomas Aquinas, the medieval doctors, and the Protestant scholastics "define divine infinity not as the endless extension of the categories of finite being, but as the transcendence of those categories." *Post-Reformation Reformed Dogmatics: The Rise and Development of Reformed Orthodoxy, ca. 1520–1725* (Grand Rapids: Baker Academic, 2003), 3:330. Note: hereafter this is referred to as *PRRD*. All categorical being is necessarily finite being as it necessarily lacks the being proper to the other categories. Older theologians were keen to point out that there can

inely infinite, God must not be composed of determinations of being more basic than His own Godhead.

Creation

The doctrine of divine creation also motivates the confession of divine simplicity. Since God is the first being from whom all other being flows, it follows that He must not derive His own being from constituent parts or elements within Himself. All things that exist in the world are said to exist by His will (Rev. 4:11). He is the one who calls that which is not as though it is (Rom. 4:17)—that is, He makes created being to exist *ex nihilo*. Additionally, it is clear that He does not employ already existing materials in creation since, as Paul states in Romans 11:36, "of Him and through Him and to Him are all things." If God should be composed of parts, then these parts would be before Him in being, even if not in time, and He would be rightly conceived of as existing *from* them or *of* them. His existence would, in some respect, be bestowed to Him as a gift He receives from another. This flouts the most fundamental biblical teaching regarding God as the all-sufficient source of all that is not identical to Him. Steven Duby observes that if God should receive His actuality of being from another, He would not "retain his ultimacy and ontic definitiveness revealed in the work of creation but would yield that ultimacy to an *esse* [i.e., act of being] back of God, a true absolute by which even God himself would be relativized."[24] When the Second London Confession 2.2 states that God is "the alone fountain of all being, of whom, through whom, and to whom are all things," it can only do so consistently so long as it also maintains that He is without parts.[25]

I have offered only a small sampling of the ways in which various biblical teachings entail the truth of God's simplicity. But it should be clear that much of the Bible's teaching about God is compromised if

---

be only one actually infinite being since if, *per impossibile*, there were two such beings one or both would have to lack being proper to the other in order to be distinguished from it. Such a privation of being would of course disqualify it from counting as actually infinite.

24. Duby, *Divine Simplicity*, 169–70.
25. Second London Confession, in Dennison, *Reformed Confessions*, 4:535.

one denies His simplicity. I will turn finally to survey the affirmation of this crucial doctrine as found in a number of prominent theologians through the ages of the church.

Historical Witness to Divine Simplicity

The Christian witness to divine simplicity enjoys a long history. At times, the articulations and defenses of it are positively beautiful and awe-inspiring. Over time, the extensive implications of the doctrine began to be worked out with increasing precision. But the basic ontological and biblical motivations remain constant.

Patristic Period

Contemplative Christian theology recognized quite early the importance of divine simplicity for maintaining God's transcendent absoluteness. The second-century pastor and apologist Irenaeus of Lyons (c. 130–202) in his famous work *Against Heresies* appeals to divine simplicity in order to prove to certain Greek emanationists that God neither exhibited passions nor underwent a mental alteration in the creation of the world: "He is a simple, uncompounded Being, without diverse members, and altogether like, and equal to Himself, since He is wholly understanding, and wholly spirit, and wholly thought, and wholly intelligence, and wholly reason, and wholly hearing, and wholly seeing, and wholly light, and the whole source of all that is good— even as the religious and pious are wont to speak concerning God."[26] Irenaeus's argument is that the Creator God confessed by Christians is not a mere demiurge who changes or begins to be what He was not in the production of the world. His simplicity, professed by the "religious and pious," certifies His absolute immutability. Irenaeus's remarks indicate that the confession of divine simplicity was not unusual among second-century Christians.

---

26. Irenaeus, *Against Heresies*, II.13.3, in *The Apostolic Fathers—Justin Martyr—Irenaeus*, vol. 1 of *The Ante-Nicene Fathers*, ed. Alexander Roberts and James Donaldson, trans. Ernest Cushing Richardson and Bernhard Pick (New York: Charles Scribner's Sons, 1903).

The fourth-century theologian Athanasius of Alexandria (c. 297–373) also argues that, as Creator of all things, God cannot be conceived to be composed of parts. The maker of the universal system cannot Himself be a system of parts: "For God is a whole and not a number of parts, and does not consist of diverse elements, but is Himself the Maker of the system of the universe. For see what impiety they utter against the Deity when they say this. For if He consists of parts, certainly it will follow that He is unlike Himself, and made up of unlike parts."[27] Parts as parts must be really distinct from each other. Athanasius's point is that a God composed of parts is made to be God from that which is somehow distinct from the totality of His deity; thus, such a thing must necessarily be a dependent being. This is impossible for God since He is the Creator of all.

Athanasius is also one of the first to conspicuously bring the truth of simplicity to bear on the doctrine of the Trinity. He argues that the Son is neither a part of God nor an offspring that came about through some change in the Godhead. He roots this conviction in God's simplicity:

> The divine generation must not be compared to the nature of men, nor the Son considered to be part of God, nor the generation to imply any passion whatever; God is not as man; for men beget passibly, having a transitive nature, which waits for periods by reason of its weakness. But with God this cannot be; for He is not composed of parts, but being impassible and simple, He is impassibly and indivisibly Father of the Son.[28]

Athanasius makes the same point in his work defending the Nicene Creed: "God, being without parts, is Father of the Son without partition or passion."[29] The assumption at the time was that in

27. Athanasius, *Against the Heathen*, 1.28, in *The Nicene and Post-Nicene Fathers*, ed. Phillip Schaff and Henry Wace, vol. 4 (Grand Rapids: Eerdmans, 1953).

28. Athanasius, *Four Discourses against the Arians*, 1.28, in *The Nicene and Post-Nicene Fathers*, ed. Phillip Schaff and Henry Wace, vol. 4 (Grand Rapids: Eerdmans, 1953).

29. Athanasius, *De Decretis or Defence of the Nicene Definition* 11, in *The Nicene and Post-Nicene Fathers*, ed. Phillip Schaff and Henry Wace, vol. 4 (Grand Rapids: Eerdmans, 1953).

generation some part of a man's substance must necessarily be divided from him in order to go forth and produce a child in his likeness. That is, he must be divisible in some regard.[30] But if God is not composed of parts, which Athanasius clearly presupposes as a baseline principle, then the Father cannot generate the Son by some abscission of His divine substance. For Athanasius, this conviction drives his doctrine of the eternal generation of the Son. Divine simplicity is clearly a controlling centerpiece of classical Christian grammar, shaping even the articulation of the Trinity.[31] In our day, it is not an uncommon claim that if divine simplicity contradicts the Trinity, then divine simplicity needs to be retooled to bring it into conformity with trinitarian teaching. In the patristic period, the order seems to have been precisely

---

30. Athanasius explains, "For the offspring of men are portions of their fathers, since the very nature of bodies is not uncompounded, but in a state of flux, and composed of parts; and men lose their substance in begetting." De Decretis or Defense of the Nicene Definition 11. While this primitive account may appear a bit naïve to modern readers, the basic notion that generation among creatures entails some sort of partition or divestment on the part of the father is not exactly false.

31. Athanasius's fourth-century Cappadocian counterparts in the defense of the Trinity—Basil of Caesarea, Gregory of Nyssa, and Gregory of Nazianzus—were also committed to the importance of divine simplicity. Gregory of Nyssa argues that the Son and the Holy Spirit could not be semidivine, as some heretics insisted, because God's simplicity proves the indivisibility of the divine essence. Only that which is composed of parts is divisible. Thus, wherever the divine essence is present it must be *wholly* present. See Gregory of Nyssa, *Against Eunomius*, bk. 10, sec. 4, and *On the Holy Spirit*, in *A Select Library of Nicene and Post-Nicene Fathers of the Christian Church: Second Series*, ed. Philip Schaff and Henry Mace, trans. William Moore and Henry Austin Wilson (Grand Rapids: Eerdmans, 1979), 5:226–27, 315–17. For a perceptive study of Basil of Caesarea and Gregory of Nyssa on this topic, see Andrew Radde-Gallwitz, *Basil of Caesarea, Gregory of Nyssa, and the Transformation of Divine Simplicity* (Oxford: Oxford University Press, 2009). Divine simplicity was also deployed by these theologians to establish the monotheistic credentials of their trinitarianism. How was one to safeguard the doctrine of the Trinity from the implication that Christians worship three gods? Lewis Ayres observes, "The deepest concern of pro-Nicene Trinitarian theology is shaping our attention to the union of the irreducible persons in the simple and unitary Godhead." *Nicaea and Its Legacy: An Approach to Fourth-Century Trinitarian Theology* (Oxford: Oxford University Press, 2004), 301. The simplicity of the Godhead is what ensures that it is not really just a corporate unity made up of beings more primitive and ontologically basic than the whole. This theme will be developed at greater length in chapter 6.

the opposite. The Trinity needed to be articulated in such a way as not to conflict with the controlling conviction of God's simplicity. Indeed, only a doctrine of simplicity could ensure that one's doctrine of the Trinity was genuinely monotheistic and that the triune God was indeed absolute in being.[32]

A final figure from the patristic period we should consider is Augustine of Hippo (354–430). Following the Cappadocian fathers, Augustine appeals to divine simplicity in his *City of God* to argue for the unchangeableness of each person of the Godhead. He writes, "It is for this reason, then, that the nature of the Trinity is called simple, because it has not anything which it can lose, and because it is not one thing and its contents another, as a cup and the liquor, or a body and its colour, or the air and the light or heat of it, or a mind and its wisdom. For none of these is what it has."[33]

In *De trinitate*, Augustine further elaborates on God's simplicity in his attempt to establish the uniqueness, independence, and singularity of the divine nature: "But it is impious to say that God subsists to and underlies his goodness, and that goodness is not his substance, or rather his being, nor is God his goodness, but it is in him as an underlying subject." This is Augustine's way of saying that all that is in God is God. He does not possess His being as creatures do, "by way of relationship with reference to something else." That which is not God does not modify or augment His being in any way. Augustine thus concludes, "So for God to be is the same as to subsist, and therefore if the Trinity is one being, it is also one substance."[34] God's attributes are not separable from His substance as so many determinations of His

---

32. See chapter 6 for a lengthier discussion of this point.

33. Augustine, *The City of God*, trans. Marcus Dods (New York: Random House, 1950), XI:10.

34. Augustine, *The Trinity*, ed. John E. Roteller, trans. Edmund Hill (Hyde Park, N. Y.: New City Press, 1991), bk. 7, 10. Augustine further affirms the identity of God's existence and essence when he writes, "What is God's knowledge is also his wisdom, and what is his wisdom is also his being or substance, because in the wonderful simplicity of that nature it is not one thing to be wise, another to be, but being wise is the same as being." *The Trinity*, bk. 15, 22. See also Lewis Ayres, *Augustine and the Trinity* (Cambridge: Cambridge University Press, 2010), 208–11.

being through which He possesses His fullness of actuality. All that God is, He is in and through Himself.

Medieval Period

In the early sixth century, Boethius (c. 480–524) appeals to divine simplicity to prove God's immutability and independence. He argues,

> But the Divine Substance is form without matter, and is therefore one, and is its own essence. But other things are not their own essences, for each thing has its being from the things of which it is composed, that is, from its parts. It is This *and* That, *i.e.* it is its parts in conjunction; it is not This *or* That taken apart.... That on the other hand which does not consist in This and That, but is only This, is really its own essence, and is altogether beautiful and stable because it does not depend upon anything.[35]

Later, in the eleventh century, Anselm of Canterbury (c. 1033–1109) praises God for His self-sufficient independency, writing in his *Proslogion*, "But clearly, you are whatever you are, not through anything else, but through yourself. Therefore, you are the very life by which you live, the wisdom by which you are wise, and the very goodness by which you are good to the good and to the wicked, and so on for similar attributes."[36] Nothing that God is can be explained by virtue of that which is not strictly identical with God. He is susceptible to no existential explanation more basic than His own Godhead. Anselm continues his prayer in the *Proslogion* by further confessing God's simplicity as the basis for His unity of being, immutability, omnipresence, and eternity:

> For whatever is composed of parts is not completely one. It is in some sense a plurality and not identical with itself, and it can be broken up either in fact or at least in the understanding. But such

---

35. Boethius, *De Trinitate*, II, 30–40, in *The Theological Tractates/The Consolation of Philosophy*, trans. H. F. Stewart, E. K. Rand, and S. J. Tester (Cambridge, Mass.: Harvard University Press, 1973).

36. Anselm, *Proslogion*, 12, in *Anselm: Basic Writings*, trans. and ed. Thomas Williams (Indianapolis: Hackett, 2007).

characteristics are foreign to you, than whom nothing greater can be thought. Therefore, there are no parts in you, Lord, and you are not a plurality. Instead, you are so much a unity, so much identical with yourself, that you are in no respect dissimilar to yourself. You are in fact unity itself; you cannot be divided by any understanding. Therefore, life and wisdom and the rest are not parts of you; they are all one. Each of them is all of what you are, and each is what the rest are. And since you have no parts, and neither does your eternity, which you yourself are, it follows that no parts of you or your eternity exists as a certain place or time. Instead, you exist as a whole everywhere, and your eternity exists as a whole always.[37]

The doctrine of God's simplicity arguably reaches its summit of expression and sophistication in the writings of Thomas Aquinas (1225–1274).[38] Several factors enabled Thomas to nuance the doctrine in ways that many of his medieval Christian predecessors had not, perhaps the most important of which was the recovery of Aristotle's metaphysical framework in which all finitude and composition is understood as a combination of principles that give actuality of being (act) and principles by which a thing receives actuality of being (passive potency). This conceptual framework did not alter the essential claims of the doctrine, though it did enable Thomas to explicate it in more precisely existential terms. In his *Compendium theologiae*, he writes:

> The first mover must be simple. For any composite being must contain two factors that are related to each other as potency to act. But in the first mover, which is altogether immobile, all combination of potency and act is impossible, because whatever is in potency is, by that very fact, movable. Accordingly the first mover cannot be composite. Moreover, something has to exist prior to any composite, since composing elements are by their very nature antecedent to a composite. Hence the first of all beings cannot

---

37. Anselm, *Proslogion*, 18.
38. For a detailed examination of Aquinas's doctrine of simplicity, see Peter Weigel, *Aquinas on Simplicity: An Investigation into the Foundations of His Philosophical Theology* (Oxford: Peter Lang, 2008).

be composite. Even within the order of composite beings we
observe that the simpler things have priority.... Hence the truth
remains that the first of beings must be absolutely simple.[39]

Thomas's argument trades on the basic truth disclosed in both nature
and Scripture that God is the absolute Creator and source of being
from whom are all things. As the ultimate giver of being, God cannot
in turn be moved to an act of being by some source more primitive
than Himself. Therefore, He must be purely actual in all that He is
and, negatively, not composed of various determinations of being.

Reformation to Present

Historian Richard Muller notes that "the underlying assumptions governing the doctrine of God during the eras of the Reformation and
Protestant orthodoxy are very little different from those governing the
discussion during the Middle Ages."[40] It is unsurprising, then, that we
find echoes of Aquinas and other medieval schoolmen in the various
Protestant articulations of the doctrine of simplicity. The early English Puritan William Perkins (1558–1602) stands in line with Anselm
and Aquinas when he explains that the "simpleness" of God's nature
means that "whatsoever is in God, is his essence, and all that he is, he
is by essence."[41] There is nothing in God that is not simply Himself,
His divinity.

John Owen (1616–1683) utilizes the doctrine of God's simplicity
in his argument against the Socinians. By it, he proves that God is the
absolute first and independent being. He writes, "Now, if God were of
any causes, internal or external, any principles antecedent or superior
to him, he could not be so absolutely first and independent. Were he
composed of parts, accidents, manner of being, he could not be first;

---

39. Thomas Aquinas, *Compendium theologiae*, ch. 9, in translation as *Compendium
of Theology*, trans. Cyril Vollert (St. Louis: B. Herder, 1947).

40. Muller, *PRRD*, 3:97.

41. William Perkins, *A Golden Chaine: or, The Description of Theology*, in *The
Workes of That Famous and Worthy Minister of Christ in the Universitie of Cambridge,
Mr. William Perkins* (London: John Legatt, 1626), 1:11. The spelling has been updated
in the citation.

all of these are before that which is of them, and therefore his essence is absolutely simple."[42] This reasoning is clearly in step with that of Thomas Aquinas. With reference to Exodus 3:14–15, Owen explains God's unity via His simplicity: "Where there is an absolute oneness and sameness in the whole, there is no composition by an union of extremes.... He, then, who is what he is, and whose all that is in him is, himself, hath neither parts, accidents, principles, nor anything else, whereof his essence should be compounded."[43] Owen's commitment to God's simplicity is typical of Reformed orthodoxy as a whole. His Continental counterpart Francis Turretin (1623–1687) declares, "The orthodox have constantly taught that the essence of God is perfectly simple and free from all composition."[44]

Herman Bavinck (1854–1921) is a more recent theologian who deserves mention. What makes his contribution significant is not its originality, but the fact that he propounds the strong classical form of divine simplicity at a time when many of his Reformed contemporaries had begun to either abandon or revise the doctrine in a direction more amenable to the demands of theistic mutualism. Bavinck skillfully and carefully spotlights the abiding significance of the classical doctrine of simplicity:

> This simplicity is of great importance...for our understanding of God. It is not only taught in Scripture (where God is called "light," "life," and "love") but also automatically follows from the idea of God and is necessarily implied in the other attributes. Simplicity here is the antonym of "compounded." If God is composed of parts, like a body, or composed of *genus* (class) and *differentiae* (attributes of differing species belonging to the same *genus*), substance and accidents, matter and form, potentiality and actuality, essence and existence, then his perfection, oneness, independence, and immutability, cannot be maintained. On that

---

42. Owen, *Vindicae Evangelicae*, in *Works*, 12:72. In sourcing previous scholarship Owen appeals first and foremost to Thomas Aquinas's *Summa contra Gentiles*.

43. Owen, *Vindicae Evangelicae*, in *Works*, 12:72.

44. Francis Turretin, *Institutes of Elenctic Theology*, ed. James T. Dennison, Jr., trans. George Musgrave Giger (Phillipsburg, N.J.: P&R, 1992), vol. 1, III.7.1.

basis he is not the highest love, for then there is in him a subject who loves—which is one thing—as well as a love by which
he loves—which is another. The same dualism would apply to
all the other attributes. In that case God is not the One "than
whom nothing better can be thought." Instead, God is uniquely
his own, having nothing above him. Accordingly, he is completely
identical with the attributes of wisdom, grace, and love, and so
on. He is absolutely perfect, the One "than whom nothing higher
can be thought."[45]

The doctrine of divine simplicity is among the most fundamental
and widely held dogmas of classical Christian theism. It is clearly central
to the collective consciousness of historical Christian thought on God.

Conclusion

The doctrine of divine simplicity is meant to correct any proclivity we
might have toward conceiving God's being as dependent on principles
or sources of being more basic than His own divinity. This temptation is very real insofar as everything else we know and experience is
composed of parts. Peter Sanlon writes, "We become so used to this
that we naturally transfer our assumptions to God. We think of God
as if he were fundamentally like his creation." But a God composed of
parts is unworthy of our worship because He is not the highest being;
rather He is something that is caused to exist by another. "Simplicity,"
Sanlon maintains, "is the doctrine that challenges us out of these idolatrous assumptions."[46]

Divine simplicity—together with its positive counterpart, divine
pure actuality—constitutes a baseline, a controlling grammar for all
our thoughts and beliefs about God. If other theological proposals
about God do not conform to this most fundamental conviction of
His existential absoluteness, which can only be consistently maintained if God is first confessed to be simple, then we run the very real
danger of worshipping that which is not the unsurpassable and most
absolute being.

---

45. Bavinck, *Reformed Dogmatics*, 2:176.
46. Sanlon, *Simply God*, 79.

CHAPTER 4

Simple God Lost

While the logic of divine simplicity may be compelling—God is most absolute in existence and so cannot depend upon that which is not God for any actuality of His being—the doctrine carries with it some deeply counterintuitive and, to some, even strange implications. Chiefly, it means that all that is in God is God. There is no distinction in Him between His act of existence and essence, between His substance and attributes, or between His nature and His intrinsic activity. All these things are nothing but God and do not exist in Him as principles or determinations of His being. From this follow some curious implications for our language about God. It means that our ordinary creaturely patterns of speech (e.g., subject + predicate) do not quite fit God in the way that they fit creatures.

An example may help illumine this point. In the statement "Albert is wise and powerful," we distinguish between the subject, "Albert," and the two terms attributed to him. Moreover, the distinctions that appear in the syntax of our language (Albert + wisdom + power) tend to mirror real distinctions in the things about which we are speaking. Albert is not identical with wisdom and power; neither are Albert's wisdom and power identical with each other. They exist together only through some power of composition. The composite form of our statement follows from the actual composition of Albert, the primary substance, with the properties of wisdom and power. In this way, the syntax of our language is a generally reliable guide or map to the shape of natural reality. Subjects and predicates, when referring to natural and composite entities, are not merely distinct as terms in our statements; the distinctions in terms reflect real distinctions in the things themselves about which we speak. The temptation is to think that since our speech generally functions this way with respect to creatures, then it must also work this way when we speak of God. But herein lies the difficulty: *a simple God is not composed of parts; thus, His being cannot be directly mapped onto any multipart statements we make about Him.*

Divine simplicity accordingly insists on an inescapable incapacity and inadequacy in all our God-talk. We can have only complex propositions and thoughts about the simple God. We cannot discover the manner of God's being by attempting to read it off the surface grammar of our propositions about Him. The shape of our propositional statements is only suited to correspond in a one-to-one manner to multipart and composite beings.

This fact about language is perhaps one of the leading motives for theistic mutualist departures from divine simplicity. If the manner of our God-talk is not a direct map of the manner of God's being, the thinking goes, then what hope is there of knowing Him as He truly is? Knowing Him as we know other persons? For many theologians, the price of confessing a simple God is too steep to pay. It is one counter-intuitive bridge too far to accept that our statements about God do not disclose His manner of being the way our statements about creatures disclose to us their manners of being. This wariness of the traditional doctrine of divine simplicity is the common feature of virtually all theistic mutualists, of open theists and Calvinists alike.

There seem to be three basic approaches taken by modern dissenters from divine simplicity. Many proceed by disregarding the doctrine. Others positively deny the doctrine. Still others distort the traditional doctrine by reconceiving it as teaching a sublime complex unity of really distinct attributes in God's essence. Each one of these approaches—disregard, denial, and distortion—holds that the supreme absoluteness of God can be preserved either by some less recondite doctrine or by a less austere version of simplicity. Yet the consistent maintenance of divine absoluteness will elude every theological approach that refuses to uphold God's absolute simplicity. Each of the views to be considered below ends up relativizing God in some way or another in order to render Him more intelligible to ordinary human ways of speaking and thinking.

Disregarding Divine Simplicity

The majority of evangelical theistic mutualists run afoul of the doctrine of God's simplicity not so much by denying it as by disregarding it. Before offering remarks on a few recent theologians, it would perhaps be useful to think briefly about how this disregard came about. It is by no means a recent trend. Prior to the eighteenth century, it would have been nearly impossible to find a work of theology proper, Catholic or Protestant, that did not give considerable attention to divine simplicity and assign to it a weighty role in the account of God's attributes. By the middle of the eighteenth century, however, the doctrine began increasingly to disappear or to be relegated to a footnote. Why is this?

One plausible explanation seems to be the emergence in Europe of new, restricted views concerning causality. The mechanistic physics of the early Enlightenment tended to disregard the traditional categories of formal and final causation, thus eclipsing a vast portion of what earlier generations would have understood causation to involve.[1] Formal causes supply any manner of "whatness" to a thing, and final causes supply the reason for a thing's development or movement in a certain direction.[2] All that remained of causality after mechanism took over

---

1. For a detailed account of how early modern mechanism displaced the older, predominantly Aristotelian, natural philosophy, see Stephen Gaukroger, *The Emergence of a Scientific Culture: Science and the Shaping of Modernity, 1210–1695* (Oxford: Clarendon, 2006), 167–69, 253–351, 457–71.

2. Generally speaking, a cause is whatever influences the being of a thing. Formal causes are those that supply "what-ness" or quiddity to things. The substantial form of caninity is what *causes* this dog to be a dog and not a cat, for example, and the substantial form of felinity is what *causes* this cat to be a cat and not anything else. The accidental form of the color brown is what *causes* the dog to be a brown dog, and the accidental form of sharpness is what *causes* the cat's claws to inflict pain—and so forth. Final causes answer the question, what is it for? Purpose, or teleology, is believed to *cause* a thing to behave as it does in development toward a certain end. The end goal of becoming an oak tree is the final goal that *causes* the acorn to germinate and grow as it does. In short, purpose is a cause of a thing's activity. We should note that it is not quite right to think of God as subject to final causality since His being and actions do not *move* toward an end of being with which He is not eternally and fully identical. God is eternally the beginning and the end. With reference to God, then, finality functions rather as a sufficient reason of God's being and actions and not properly as a cause of being.

the field of natural philosophy was a mechanical or physicalist under-standing of efficient and material causation. Efficient causality was, to put it crassly, reduced to bits of matter producing movement and change in other bits of matter by pushing or pulling them. And mate-rial causality was regarded merely as the physical stuff that causes a body to have its particular material characteristics and to thus behave in certain ways respective to that material constitution. How did these changing perspectives on causality affect Christian commitment to the doctrine of God's simplicity?

The aim of divine simplicity is to deny all relativity in God and to show that God's being is ontologically irreducible in every respect. This work of negation is meant to ensure that we do not undermine God's perfect absoluteness—that is, His infinite fullness of being as the one behind whom there can be no deeper explanation or cause of being. There is nothing deeper or more fundamental in being than divinity, nothing more absolute. If divine simplicity is meant to ensure that God's being is not relative but absolute, then a significant part of its work is to deny that God's being follows in any way from a cause. But if one loses the robust proper understanding of what counts as a cause, or how causes operate in the production of a thing's being, then it will no longer be clear exactly what important work divine simplicity performs. The restricted understanding of causality in the Enlight-enment era and subsequent periods tended to result in a restricted understanding of the meaning and significance of divine simplicity as well. The doctrine of simplicity had much less work to do once entire categories of causation began to disappear from popular and philo-sophical thought.

Another possible reason for the decline in attention to divine sim-plicity is due to the newfound skepticism of David Hume (1711–1776), who argued that humans can have no knowledge of causal necessity. We simply cannot have a sense experience of necessary causes, and thus all talk about causation is mere speculation, not knowledge. For Hume, a belief in causal necessity is simply a psychological response to the uniformity of our experience. Immanuel Kant (1724–1804) responded to Hume's skepticism by insisting that causality is a rela-tion that we impose on the things of our sense experience. But like the

Enlightenment physics that preceded them, neither Kant nor Hume allowed a place for formal and final causes. Moreover, their approach relegated metaphysics from an examination of the world to an examination of one's concepts about the world, from the study of being to the study of thought. Hume famously recommended consigning books of "school metaphysics," which contained nothing but "sophistry and illusion," to the flames. Kant ruled out the possibility of natural man knowing substantial or accidental forms and thus was critical of the entire theory of being and becoming that had grown up around the assumption that one could know such things.

The effect of Hume's skepticism and Kant's "critical" revolution on theological language and articulation should not be underestimated. The medieval scholastic theologians, as well as the seventeenth-century Protestant scholastics who followed them, had articulated the doctrine of simplicity in terms of an elaborate scheme of denials in which the four causes known through Aristotelian metaphysics (final, formal, efficient, and material) were carefully denied of God. But one would need to presuppose the basic accuracy of Aristotelian metaphysics (or at least that version of it as modified by Aquinas and others) for such elaborate denials to continue to make sense. After Hume and Kant's attack on the perennial Aristotelian philosophy, many a Christian theologian opted to abandon, rather than defend, the metaphysical structure (regarding being, becoming, and causation) in terms of which simplicity had been so meticulously developed. Indeed, many Christian theologians and ministers retreated from the field of metaphysics altogether and retrenched themselves in their Bibles, assuming that the Bible's teaching could be successfully preserved without committing oneself to a particular understanding of being.

One might wonder how the doctrine of divine simplicity survived this Enlightenment onslaught of mechanism, skepticism, and critical theory. The fact is that it has not fared well over the past three centuries. Nevertheless, the older approach to being has not become entirely extinct. One place it survives even today is in the theological literature from the pre-Enlightenment era and in the many confessions of faith that were produced by the churchmen of that era. The older, more robust understanding of being and becoming has also continued into the twentieth and twenty-first centuries in the work of Reformed theologians such as Herman Bavinck and Louis Berkhof, numerous Catholic scholars (mostly neo-Thomists), and more recently in philosophical-theological defenses such as those of Brian Davies and Steven Duby. In these works, the doctrine still confronts modern readers. But this does not mean that modern readers actually understand the claims of the doctrine. By and large, most have progressively lost sight of the significance of the older and more elaborately textured causal language. In post-Enlightenment thought, terms such as we find in the medieval schoolmen and classical Protestant confessions—like "parts," "passions," and "substance"—are no longer regarded with their original intent and richness. Indeed, after the Enlightenment the denial of parts in God was increasingly taken to mean merely that God lacks material parts. This explanation is offered, for instance, by a number of post-Enlightenment Protestant theologians including A. A. Hodge, J. Oliver Buswell, and more recently Robert Reymond.[3] Such a restricted understanding of parts as material quantities betrays just how much the mechanistic Enlightenment thinking has impacted Christian theology. This constrained way of thinking about simplicity makes it all too easy to politely dismiss the doctrine. Beyond the obvious denial that God is comprised of material bits, it is no longer clear what role divine simplicity is supposed to play in our understanding of God.

This brings us to the recent disregard of the doctrine. In many ways it seems to be in step with the trajectory of much of evangelical Protestant thought since the eighteenth century. Thus, it may not strike us as particularly daring, dangerous, or even very significant.

---

3. See A. A. Hodge, *The Confession of Faith* (1869; repr., London: Banner of Truth Trust, 1958), 47, 49; Buswell, *Systematic Theology*, 1:56; Robert L. Reymond, *A New Systematic Theology of the Christian Faith* (Nashville: Thomas Nelson, 1998), 167. It is difficult to say just how self-conscious each of these theologians is in overlooking the original intent of Westminster divines on this point. Hodge elsewhere seems to have some sense of the original intent derived from his reading of Francis Turretin. It is peculiar that he omits this in his exposition of the Westminster Confession. See A. A. Hodge, *Outlines of Theology* (1879; repr., Edinburgh: Banner of Truth Trust, 1972), 136–37.

Nevertheless, I would contend that the disregard of the doctrine has opened the door for the theological way of thinking that predominates in theistic mutualism. The end result is a relativization of the being of God. One does not need a background in Thomistic metaphysics to see that this is the case.

I shall confine my focus to one particular dismissal of divine simplicity that shows itself in the thinking of evangelical theistic mutualists—namely, the assumption that in God there are some attributes that belong to His essence, while there are other attributes He acquires through relation with His creatures. These He possesses in addition to His essence. This violates divine simplicity's insistence that God cannot be composed of substance and accidents, though most theistic mutualists would not use such terminology.[4] Where exactly do we find such teaching?

Let us again consider Bruce Ware's doctrine of God's relational mutability mentioned in chapter 2. Ware writes, "God changes from anger to mercy, from blessing to cursing, from rejection to acceptance. *Each of these changes is real in God*, though no such change affects in the slightest the unchangeable supremacy of his intrinsic nature."[5] This way of putting things clearly assumes that there are realities in God by which God exists in some particular way (as angry, merciful, blessing, cursing, rejecting, or accepting) that are not themselves identical with the reality of His nature. By "nature," I take Ware to mean the divine essence or substantial form. We might rightly conclude, then, that for Ware the reality of God's so-called dispositions or attitudes is an actuality of being in Him that is not identical with His divine

---

4. An "accident" is anything that adds some actuality of being to a subject (the primary substance) that the subject does not already possess in virtue of its essence (i.e., its substantial form). These accidents are sources of being really distinct from a subject's essence. Thus, some aspects of a subject's being are caused (i.e., made to be actual) in virtue of its essence, and others are caused in it in virtue of its accidents. Obviously, any such subject is a being composed of both substantial form (essence) and accidental determinations of being. For the denial that God can be composed of substance and accident see Aquinas, *Summa theologiae* Ia.3.6. See also Dolezal, *God without Parts*, 58–62. Thomas's denial is reproduced by the vast majority of seventeenth-century Protestant scholastics who write on this topic.

5. Ware, "Evangelical Reformulation," 440–41. Emphasis added.

essence or nature as such. They cannot be aspects of His nature since Ware insists that these realities change, while the divine nature cannot. Thus, there is something real in God and by which He *exists* in a certain way—something that is not itself God or divinity, namely, the accidental actuality of His alleged dispositions.[6] This feature relativizes the being of God to just the extent it entails that some aspect of His existence—the existential state of His *being* angry or merciful, and of His intrinsic *acting* to bless, curse, reject, or accept—is ultimately accounted for by something other than the actuality of His divinity. On this scheme, not all that is in God is God. Ware's way of describing God's being is only possible so long as the claims of divine simplicity are disregarded.[7]

Ware's assumptions about the divine being may not appear novel or exotic inasmuch as several, perhaps even a majority, of contemporary evangelical theologians operate on the same assumptions. Rob Lister, for example, speaks of God as responding to creatures in such a way that it involves "a transition that occurs in God."[8] This movement in God is from one state of activity or feeling to another. According to Lister, there are "certain divine attributes and…certain dispositions of passion that God takes on in respect to his creation."[9] These are taken

---

6. Ware complains that process theism makes God's existence to depend upon "some form of reality other than God." See "Evangelical Reformulation," 435. Yet strangely Ware does precisely this same thing when he makes the existential state of God's "dispositions" and "attitudes" depend upon some form of affective reality other than His own eternal, divine nature. Remember, for Ware, these are states of mind, affection, or action in God that are not identical with the divine nature itself.

7. Ware affirms the ontological immutability of the divine nature. See, for example, "Evangelical Reformulation," 435; *God's Lesser Glory*, 73; *God's Greater Glory*, 140–45. The problem with his account lies in his insistence that God is ontologically immutable and yet undergoes real, intrinsic changes of attitude and disposition. This is tantamount to saying there are realities in God that do not fall under the consideration of what is. But nothing can be real and fail to count as ontological since ontology studies being and existence (is-ness). Unfortunately, this sort of confusion with respect to the language of being abounds in the God-talk of many modern evangelicals.

8. Lister, *God Is Impassible and Impassioned*, 179.

9. Lister, *God Is Impassible and Impassioned*, 225. In contrast, classical theism would insist that whatever comes to be in time, such as an acquired property of being, is necessarily finite and should not be regarded as divine in any sense.

on in addition to the divine nature, which Lister believes is eternal and unchanging in God. Thus, like Ware, he assumes a real distinction in God between God's nature and the determinations of His "emotions" or activities with respect to creation. In order to propose such a scheme for the divine attributes, Lister is forced to set aside—whether intentionally or not—the doctrine of God's simplicity. This opens the way for him to affirm that God acquires being that He does not eternally possess in His essence. As with all theistic mutualists, Lister's purpose in this is to explain God's relation to the world as one of genuine give-and-take and in which God is *really* affected by His creatures. But in reasoning this way, it follows that God's existential absoluteness is necessarily forfeited. Nevertheless, I suspect that many who theologize in this manner are truly unaware of the implications in this regard.

Denying Divine Simplicity

While many evangelical theistic mutualists transgress the doctrine of simplicity through perhaps unintentional disregard of it, others have set themselves in direct and clear opposition to the doctrine. The late Ronald Nash is one recent evangelical theologian and philosopher who denies the usefulness of divine simplicity. He believes that "human beings could never have knowledge of any absolutely simple essence."[10] Only composite beings can be accessed in a direct way by our speech and knowledge, and only such direct one-to-one access enables us to know the truth. For Nash, all human language must have a bijective function that enables us to directly map the manner of a thing's being based on the form of propositions about that thing. All language, regardless of its object being natural or supernatural, functions as a mirror of those things to which it refers. Suggesting that humans know God by way of analogy does not ease Nash's concerns. "If human beings necessarily conceive God differently than He really is," he asks, "is their conception of God not therefore false?"[11]

---

10. Nash, *Concept of God*, 85.
11. Nash, *Concept of God*, 86.

Nash's second objection to simplicity follows philosopher Alvin Plantinga's critique of Thomas Aquinas on this topic.[12] On the Thomist doctrine of simplicity, Nash observes that each one of God's properties is identical with all the others. This seems to require that God has really only one property. Nash objects that this is mystifying. While he is willing to acknowledge that many things about God are incomprehensible to us, the notion of property identity cannot be one of them. This is, according to him, because "one of the things we do seem to know very clearly is that power and love and knowledge and mercy are not identical properties."[13]

Nash's third objection also follows Plantinga. He claims that if God should be identical with His properties, then it would turn out that God just is a property. But a property is an abstract object and cannot possibly be a person, who has knowledge and who creates (as the God of the Bible does). Furthermore, Nash alleges that if God should be a property, then it would lead "to the odd suggestion that the biblical teaching that God is characterized by a variety of distinct properties is wrong."[14] With this we come full circle. What Nash intends is that a simple God appears not to exist in a manner directly equivalent to the manner in which human speech refers to Him.

Nash reckons that the liabilities of divine simplicity are too much to bear since they demand conclusions "that conflict with other important tenets of Christian theism." Presumably by this he means the Christian belief that God is a personal being who has knowledge and carries out intentional actions. "It would appear," Nash concludes, "that Christian theologians have no good reason to affirm the doctrine of divine simplicity. It seems doubtful that the doctrine adds anything significant to our understanding of God."[15]

---

12. Alvin Plantinga, *Does God Have a Nature?* (Milwaukee, Wis.: Marquette University Press, 1980). It should be noted that the Thomist version of the doctrine of simplicity was widely maintained by the Reformed scholastics of the sixteenth and seventeenth centuries.

13. Nash, *Concept of God*, 94.

14. Nash, *Concept of God*, 95.

15. Nash, *Concept of God*, 95.

John Feinberg is another evangelical theologian who agrees with Nash (and with Plantinga) on the wrongheadedness of simplicity. His chief concern is that the doctrine does not appear to be warranted by Scripture. In fact, if anything, the Bible seems to affirm the opposite—that God really does possess attributes in distinction from His essence, and thus God appears to be composite on some level. Why does this ordinary biblical way of speaking about God not count as evidence against the argument that He is identical with all His attributes? In other words, Feinberg, like Nash, wants to know why we cannot straightforwardly read the ontological structure of God's being directly off of the surface grammar of Scripture. Even if that cannot be done, Feinberg suggests that the lack of explicit biblical data for divine simplicity "should be disconcerting at the least, and a good argument against it at most."[16] After rehearsing different aspects of the common philosophical objection that simplicity renders God an impersonal abstract property, Feinberg concludes, "These philosophical problems plus the biblical considerations…lead me to conclude that simplicity is not one of the divine attributes."[17]

These serious charges against the doctrine of simplicity warrant a few remarks in response. First, to insist that our language cannot convey to us the truth about God unless it refers to God in precisely the same manner as it refers to creatures does not appear to be the assumption of the Bible itself. Scripture teaches that God is incomprehensible in His being, and thus it would seem that we have good biblical reasons *not* to expect human language to capture His being in some one-to-one isomorphic fashion. Psalm 145:3 testifies that God's greatness is unsearchable or unfathomable. This is not merely a quantitative

---

16. John S. Feinberg, *No One Like Him: The Doctrine of God* (Wheaton, Ill.: Crossway, 2001), 329.

17. Feinberg, *No One Like Him*, 335. The evangelical philosophers J. P. Moreland and William Lane Craig tend to agree with Feinberg, declaring simplicity "a radical doctrine that enjoys no biblical support and even is at odds with the biblical conception of God in various ways." They are concerned that divine simplicity leaves us "in a state of genuine agnosticism about the nature of God." *Philosophical Foundations for a Christian Worldview* (Downers Grove, Ill.: IVP Academic, 2003), 524.

unsearchableness, but most especially a qualitative one.[18] Romans 11:33 says God's judgments and ways are unsearchable and inscrutable. According to Solomon in 1 Kings 8:27, the heaven of heavens cannot contain God, and so neither can the temple Solomon has built for God. Yet if the finite cannot contain the infinite, why should we expect complex propositions, which are designed to mirror composite and thus finite beings, to adequately measure or map the ontological structure of the infinite God? "God is love" (1 John 4:8), and "God is light" (1:5), for example, are multipart statements that should not be read as signaling some composition between God and love, or God and light. Love and light are not virtues really distinct from God that are added to Him. The complex shape of the statements, accordingly, does not mirror the *manner* of God being love or light.

As for truly knowing God, analogical revelation no more leaves us without the true knowledge of Him than the condescended manner of God's dwelling in the form of shekinah glory in Solomon's temple left the people of Israel without His true presence. The manner of His revealed presence was there accommodated to the natural, perceptive powers of His people. Thus, likewise is the manner of His revelation in the propositional statements of the Bible accommodated to the cognitive and linguistic powers of the humans to whom God speaks. God packages the disclosure of His infinite being under the form of that which is finite in order that His finite creatures may draw near to Him. James Henley Thornwell rightly insists that God's "infinite perfections are veiled under finite symbols. It is only the shadow of them that falls upon the human understanding."[19] This is true both of the phenomenal symbols of nature that God deploys as well as the propositional symbols of language. The temple and the shekinah glory

---

18. In this connection, see Steven D. Boyer and Christopher A. Hall, *The Mystery of God: A Theology for Knowing the Unknowable* (Grand Rapids: Baker Academic, 2012), 31. Boyer and Hall convincingly make the case that the mystery of God's being is not primarily extensive mystery (that there is quantitatively more to His being than we currently know), but dimensional mystery (that the *manner* of His being is not such that we can form a one-to-one concept of it).

19. James Henley Thornwell, *The Collected Writings of James Henley Thornwell* (Edinburgh: Banner of Truth Trust, 1986), 1:118.

could not adequately measure the God who dwells in unapproachable light and whom no man has seen or can see (1 Tim. 6:16). So also the articulated propositional form of Scripture's language cannot adequately measure the simple manner of God's infinite existence.

Second, and more briefly, the accusation that divine simplicity renders God an abstract property has it exactly backward. Rather than saying that God is a property, what simplicity really entails is that His so-called properties do not inhere in Him as properties. Rather, they are in fact nothing but the concrete, personal God Himself.[20] As for the distinctions we make among the attributes of God, these simply follow from the accommodated and apportioned manner by which God has divulged something of the fullness of His being to finite creatures. The distinctions are in the manner of revelation, not in God's manner of being. Thus, it turns out that divine simplicity does not leave God as an impersonal abstract object without knowledge or the power to act with intention. This removes the most compelling objection of Nash and Feinberg.

Distorting Divine Simplicity

There is a third group of modern evangelicals—those who do not undermine divine simplicity by disregarding or denying it, but by reconceiving it in a way that distorts its true meaning and significance. Many of these theologians belong to churches or schools that require subscription to one or another of the classical Reformed confessions. Accordingly, they may feel the pressure to explicitly affirm God's simplicity in ways that nonconfessional evangelicals do not.

We must first note that many of the revisionists affirm important aspects of the classical doctrine, such as the identity of God, with His existence, essence, and attributes. John Frame, for instance,

---

20. Adherents to the classical doctrine of simplicity generally deny that God has properties of being in the proper sense. Francis Turretin, for instance, writes, "Attributes are not ascribed to God properly as something superadded to his essence (something accidental to the subject), making it perfect and really distinct from himself; but improperly and transumptively inasmuch as they indicate perfections essential to the divine nature *conceived by us as properties*." *Institutes of Elenctic Theology*, vol. 1, III.5.2. Emphasis added.

writes, "Since God has no accidents, everything in him is essential to his being. So he is, in a sense, his essence."[21] Kevin Vanhoozer similarly states, "God does not 'have' properties or perfections…that stand over against or above him…. Divine simplicity stipulates that God's essence is identical with his existence."[22] On the face of it, these affirmations are wholly consistent with the classical doctrine, and one might wonder wherein the departure from the traditional view lies.

The trouble arises when we discover that the revisionists do not believe that the divine essence *itself* is simple. Vanhoozer insists that while God's attributes or properties are "coextensive," this does not mean "that all God's properties are identical with one another."[23] Frame maintains that God's attributes "all refer to his essence, but they describe different aspects of it. God really is good *and* just *and* omniscient. The multiple attributes refer to genuine complexities in his essence."[24] Frame believes that conjunctions in our statements about God pick out real conjunctions of attributes and so real distinctions in the divine essence itself. He is concerned to avoid the odd claim that the attributes of God are all synonymous. Yet the only way he can conceive of doing this is to assume that the nonsynonymous complexity of terms in our language directly maps out a corresponding complexity of being in the divine essence. Indeed, Frame has great confidence in the ability of human thought and language to adequately represent the being of God. "God," he writes, "is as clearly revealed to us, and as clearly known to us, as any created thing." Accordingly, he continues, "we need not be afraid of saying that some of our language about God is univocal or literal. God has given us language that literally applies to him."[25] Frame means not only that the truth of our propositions corresponds to the reality of God's nature, but that the *form* of our propositions mirrors the *form* or *manner* of God's intrinsic act of being. Frame is by no means alone in his univocist claims, as similar

---

21. John M. Frame, *The Doctrine of God* (Phillipsburg, N.J.: P&R, 2002), 226.

22. Kevin J. Vanhoozer, *Remythologizing Theology: Divine Action, Passion, and Authorship* (Cambridge: Cambridge University Press, 2010), 274–75.

23. Vanhoozer, *Remythologizing Theology*, 275.

24. Frame, *Doctrine of God*, 229.

25. Frame, *Doctrine of God*, 208–9.

remarks can be found in older Calvinist theologians such as Charles Hodge and R. L. Dabney and, more recently, in Robert Reymond.[26]

How does the notion of a complex divine essence distort the classical doctrine of simplicity? In short, it reconceives the unity of the divine essence as a corporate unity comprised of more basic units of actuality and intelligibility.[27] No particular attribute is ontologically identical to the divine essence as such. This relativizes the being of God by making His essence to depend on principles or sources of being which are not strictly identical with it. On this scheme, something other than divinity makes divinity to be. When Frame says

26. Charles Hodge writes, "To say, as the schoolmen, and so many even of Protestant theologians, ancient and modern, were accustomed to say, that the divine attributes differ only in name, or in our conceptions, or in their effects, is to destroy all true knowledge of God." He adds, "Knowledge is no more identical with power in God than it is in us. Thought in him is no more creative than thought in us." *Systematic Theology* (Grand Rapids: Eerdmans, 1952), 1:371–72. R. L. Dabney asserts that

> reason forbids us to think of different attributes as identical. We intuitively know that thought is not conation, and conation is not sensibility; it is impossible to think these actually identical in God as in ourselves.... The Bible always speaks of God's attributes as distinct, and yet not dividing his unity; of his intelligence and will as different; of his wrath, love, pity, wisdom, as not the same activities of the Infinite Spirit. We are taught that each of these is inconceivably higher than the principle in man which bears the corresponding name; but if the Scriptures do not mean to teach us that they are distinguishable in God, as truly as in man, and that this is as consistent as his being an infinite monad as with our souls being finite monads, then they are unmeaning.

Discussions, vol. 1, *Theological and Evangelical* (1890; repr., Harrisonburg, Va.: Sprinkle Publications, 1982), 1:290. Robert Reymond holds the same: "For surely God's eternality is no more identical with his knowledge, his knowledge no more identical with his power, his power no more identical with his omnipresence, and his omnipresence no more identical with his holiness than is our knowledge identical with our power or our goodness identical with our finite extension in space. God's attributes are real, distinguishable characteristics of his divine being." *New Systematic Theology of the Christian Faith*, 163.

27. Herman Bavinck faults Charles Hodge's doctrine of real attribute distinction in God by observing that it assumes "an objective difference in God at the expense of his simplicity and immutability." *Reformed Dogmatics*, 2:119. We may safely conclude that this same critique would apply to those other Calvinist theologians past and present who concur with Hodge.

that God is His essence, he means that God is identical to the *summative set* of really distinct properties which collectively comprise His essence.[28] The essence as a whole is evidently ontologically reducible to the particular, distinct attributes that comprise it. This is rather unlike a doctrine of divine simplicity.

The classical doctrine of simplicity denies that God's attributes are really distinct in Him.[29] The reasoning is that if God is identical

---

28. The complex-essence view seems to regard God's divinity as a sum of discrete properties. And any sum whole must depend upon parts that are not strictly identical with it. Consider Reymond's endorsement of this collective or summative understanding of God's essence or nature: "By the term *nature* I refer to the complex of attributes or characteristics that belongs to or inheres in any given entity and makes it to be what it is in distinction from everything else.... It is precisely in the *sum total* of [God's] attributes that his essence as God finds expression.... Without them, either collectively or singly, he would simply cease to be God." *New Systematic Theology of the Christian Faith*, 161. This would be agreeable if all Reymond meant was that God's essence can lack none of those virtues we attribute to Him. And surely he means at least this much. But his point also appears decidedly ontological in that he seems to be saying God has His essence as the sum result of inhering properties, each singly contributing something to the whole. If this is what Reymond's position comes to, then God's essence is a bundle of more basic or primitive causes of being and is thus dependent on that which is less than the whole to be the whole that it is. This is radically at odds with the confession of both God's simplicity and absoluteness.

29. Consider again the words of John Owen cited in the previous chapter: "*The attributes of God, which alone seem to be distinct things in the essence of God, are all of them essentially the same with one another, and every one the same with the essence of God itself.*" *Vindicae Evangelicae*, in *Works*, 12:72. Swinnock also affirms the real identity of God's attributes in Him, writing, "His justice is his mercy, and his wisdom is his patience, and his knowledge is his faithfulness, and his mercy is his justice, &c. Though they are distinguished in regard of their objects, and in regard of our apprehensions of them, and in regard of their effects, yet they are all one in themselves; and this floweth from the former head, because they are the essence of God, and his essence is a pure undivided being." *Incomparableness of God*, in *Works*, 4:423. This attribute-identity version of divine simplicity appears to have been the Reformed consensus in the seventeenth century. William Twisse, the first moderator of the Westminster Assembly, remarked, "That Gods attributes are not really distinguished, we all confess." *A Discovery of D. Jacksons Vanitie* (London: N.p., 1631), 74. Turretin helpfully distills the basic concern of the classical attribute-identity account of simplicity: "The attributes of God cannot really differ from his essence or from one another (as one thing from another) because God is most simple and perfect. Now a real distinction presupposes things diverse in essence which the highest simplicity rejects. Things really diverse can become one only by aggregation (which is opposed to absolute perfection). Again, if

with His own act of being, then He cannot depend on a multitude of really distinct causes of that being. And that is precisely how properties or attributes function in the entities in which they inhere. They are determinations of being which are distinct from the whole and which cause those things that exhibit or exemplify them to *be* in some way or another. The illustration given at the beginning of this chapter of a wise and powerful man may help illumine this point. Possessing the property of wisdom is that by virtue of which Albert is actually wise. The property of power is that by virtue of which he is actually powerful. These attributes are really distinct in the subject insofar as they are really discrete determinations of being in him. Wisdom makes Albert to be wise, and power makes him to be powerful. But Albert could be wise and lack power, or powerful and lack wisdom. This is because among creatures power and wisdom are not the same property and thus function as discrete determinations of the creature's actuality. But in God there is no such distinction inasmuch as that by virtue of which He is wise is simply His divinity and that by virtue of which He is powerful is the selfsame divinity—and so on for all His other attributes. There can be no real composition or aggregation of virtues if all are just one and the same reality—namely, divinity itself. *God's essence, being simple, in no way follows from a composition or aggregation of His attributes.*

So what are we to make of the accusation that the older attribute-identity version of simplicity renders all of God's attributes synonymous and thus all our talk about Him meaningless? Frame, for example, believes that Aquinas's insistence on the identity of the divine attributes in God means that God is a being "for whom any language suggesting complexity, distinctions, or multiplicity, is entirely unsuited."[30] But we must ask, unsuited for what? It is true that the older advocates of God's simplicity held that our language is not suited to disclose the manner of God's existence to us in a comprehensible one-to-one fashion. But

they differed really, the essence would be made perfect by something really distinct from itself and so could not be in itself most perfect." *Institutes of Elenctic Theology*, vol. 1, III.5.7.

30. Frame, *Doctrine of God*, 227.

there are other suitable ways in which the complexity of our language may refer to God truthfully. For instance, Aquinas and the Reformed scholastics held that in God's effects the perfection of His undivided essence is shown forth in a vast array of creaturely perfections. Accordingly, what is a simple unity in God is presented to the human knower under the form of creaturely multiplicity. But this refraction of His simple glory into so many beams of finite perfection does not mean these multifarious beams speak no truth about His simple nature.[31] They just do not speak that truth under the incomprehensible simple form of that nature.

Part of the language difficulty is that we draw everything that we say about God from the images and vestiges of Him found in creation. Thus, the shape of our speech about God is in some unavoidable way contoured by the shape of those complex creaturely things from which we derive our thoughts and language. Bavinck most helpfully reminds us of this:

> It must not be overlooked that we have no knowledge of God other than from his revelation in the creaturely world.... Of God we have no direct but only an indirect kind of knowledge, a concept derived from the creaturely world. Though not exhaustive, it is not untrue, since all creatures are God's creatures and therefore display something of his perfections.... Scripture, which is theological through and through and derives all things from God, over and over in its method of knowing nevertheless — or rather because of this — ascends to God from a position in the world (Isa. 40:26; Rom. 1:20). Precisely because everything comes from God, everything points back to God. All who think about him or want to speak about him derive — whether by way

---

31. The Puritan Thomas Watson states that God's attributes "are the beams by which his divine nature shines forth." *A Body of Divinity* (London: Banner of Truth Trust, 1958), 48. Similarly, Swinnock explains that God's various attributes "are all one and the same; as when the sunbeams shine through a yellow glass they are yellow, a green glass they are green, a red glass they are red, and yet all the while the beams are the same." *Incomparableness of God*, in *Works*, 4:423–24. This imagery of God's attributes as a refracted, multicolored display of His simple essence is a common one in Augustinian and Thomist theology proper.

of affirmation or negation—the forms and images needed for that purpose from the world around them.[32]

The only creaturely language suitable to express the simple God is a complex language since the only language that can be used by us to refer to God is drawn from the world of finite, complex beings.[33] It is under the form of the finite that God reveals His infinite perfection. The diversity of divine attributes lies, then, on the side of God's *revelation* to creatures, not in the being of God Himself. George Swinnock states, "God's attributes are one most pure essence diversely apprehended of us, as it is diversely manifested to us."[34] The mistake of

---

32. Bavinck, *Reformed Dogmatics*, 2:130.

33. As Aquinas explains, "We can speak of simple things only as though they were like the composite things from which we derive our knowledge. Therefore in speaking of God, we use concrete nouns to signify His subsistence, because with us only those things subsist which are composite; and we use abstract nouns to signify His simplicity. In saying therefore that Godhead, or life, or the like are in God, we indicate the composite way in which our intellect understands, but not that there is any composition in God." *Summa theologiae* Ia.3.3, ad 1. For a technical treatment of the accommodated character of our language about God see Gregory P. Rocca, *Speaking the Incomprehensible God: Thomas Aquinas on the Interplay of Positive and Negative Theology* (Washington, D.C.: Catholic University of America Press, 2004). Though Rocca primarily considers Thomas, his volume is arguably one of the most articulate and detailed guides available for understanding the assumptions about theological language that would have typified the Reformed scholastic successors of Thomas.

34. Swinnock, *Incomparableness of God*, in *Works*, 4:423. The Particular Baptist theologian John Gill is strikingly lucid on this point:

Every attribute of God is God himself, is his nature, and are only so many ways of considering it, or are so many displays of it.... Nor is [simplicity] to be disproved by the attributes of God; for they are no other than God himself, *and neither differ from one another*, but with respect to their objects and effects, and in our manner of conception of them.... They are himself, and his nature; he is not only eternal, wise, good, loving, &c. but he is eternity itself, wisdom itself, goodness itself, love itself, &c. and these are not parts of his nature, but displays of the same undivided nature, and are different considerations of it, in which we view it; our minds being so weak as not to be able to conceive of God at once and together, and in the gross, but one thing after another, and the same in different lights, that we may better understand it: these several things called attributes, *which are one in God*, are predicated of him, and ascribed to him distinctly, for helps to our finite understandings, and for the relief of our minds; and that we, with more facility and ease,

those who insist upon a complex divine essence is in expecting human language and thought to parallel the very form of God's being. This is impossible since all our thought and language is drawn from creation, and the creation cannot measure the Creator. Ultimately, the retooled doctrine of simplicity upheld by the revisionists is really just another version of divine complexity and so is not worthy of the name "simplicity."[35] The unintended yet still very real consequence of the complex-essence doctrine is to subvert the ontological absoluteness of God's divinity.

Conclusion

No doubt the theistic mutualists we have evaluated in this survey sincerely believe God to be the alone worthy object of our worship and desire to uphold the absoluteness of His being. Yet in their various detractions from the doctrine of divine simplicity, they have opened the door for the erosion of the very divine absoluteness they profess. If we are to faithfully preserve the infinite and unsurpassable glory of God's being, we will have to recover the older commitment to divine simplicity and the incomprehensibility of God and forsake the misguided path of thinking that our thought or language adequately computes the mysterious manner of God's existence.

---

might conceive of the nature of God, and take in more of him, as we can by parcels and piecemeals, than in the whole.... All those attributes are only intellectual notions; by which are conceived the perfections that are in the essence of God, but in reality are nothing but his essence.

A Body of Divinity (Grand Rapids: Sovereign Grace Publishers, 1971), 33–34. Emphasis mine. In other words, the "diversity" of God's attributes lies on the side of divine revelation and man's way of considering that revelation, not in God's very nature as such. By the terms "together," "gross," and "whole," Gill is merely speaking imprecisely. He clearly does not mean to intimate that God's nature is an aggregate of His attributes.

35. Frame appears close to conceding this when he writes, "Since simplicity in this sense [of complexity within the divine nature] does not rule out all multiplicity, it might be less confusing to use the term *necessary existence* rather than simplicity." *Doctrine of God*, 227.

CHAPTER 5

Eternal Creator

While the doctrine of divine eternity is commonly confessed, it is undoubtedly among the most difficult theological claims to understand. God is the King eternal (1 Tim. 1:17), the Alpha and the Omega (Rev. 1:8), the One whose years have no end (Ps. 102:27), who is from everlasting to everlasting (Ps. 90:2). He exists exalted above all time (2 Tim. 1:9; Titus 1:2) as Creator and Lord and does not have His life or existence computed and measured out to Him in increments of succession.[1] Rather, as His simplicity demands, He is perfectly identical with all that is in Himself. Yet the Lord of time both reveals Himself and unfolds His sovereign purpose in time.[2] All our knowledge of Him arises from our standpoint within the temporal flow of the created order. We come to know Him and speak of Him as He reveals Himself through His mighty deeds and words, one after another in succession. For this reason, we find it impossible to speak of a timeless God without employing time-bound terminology. Indeed, as with our

---

1. Both 2 Timothy 1:9 and Titus 1:2 describe God's purposeful activity as πρὸ χρόνων αἰωνίων. Literally rendered "before times eternal" or "above times eternal," the sense is that God's intrinsic activity is not a temporally indexed event. In the context, the point is that God's good purposes toward His people are not an afterthought with Him, but are eternally settled apart from the fluctuations of history.

2. Properly considered, time is not an entity or an essence but rather is a relation between things that change and are liable to change. Time is concreated with all creatures insofar as it is the measure and the numbering of all their movement. When we speak of time as a realm, we do not mean to imply that it is like a container or box in which temporal things exist; rather, we denote simply the created order which is populated by beings that are subject to and undergo change and thus are measured temporally.

talk about all God's attributes, there is an acute nonsymmetry between the temporally shaped terms and concepts we use to describe His eternity and the ontological reality of that eternity in Him.

Augustine of Hippo, who wrote so profoundly of time and eternity in his famous *Confessions*, is a wonderful example of one who aims to speak of divine eternity and yet finds himself unable to escape the terminology of time: "Your years do not come and go. Our years pass and new ones arrive only so that all may come in turn, but your years stand all at once, because they are stable: there is no pushing out of vanishing years by those that are coming on, because with you none are transient…. Your today does not give way to tomorrow, nor follow yesterday. Your Today is eternity."[3] The Puritan John Owen rightly recognizes God's eternity as a great mystery:

> How inconceivable is this glorious divine property unto the thoughts and minds of men! How weak are the ways and terms whereby they go about to express it…. He that says most only signifies what he knows of what it is not. We are of yesterday, change every moment, and are leaving our station to-morrow. God is still the same, was so before the world was,—from eternity. And now I cannot think what I have said, but only have intimated what I adore.[4]

Although it is incomprehensible in itself, this great mystery of God's eternity does not leave us speechless. It seems that we at least know how *not* to characterize eternity—to wit, our God-talk must eschew any notion of change in God. Whatever we are to say of God's work in the world—creation, judgment, redemption, consummation— we must insist that this work produces no change in Him.

This inevitably brings the classical doctrine of divine eternity into conflict with the basic demands of theistic mutualism. Theistic mutualists reason that if God is to be really related to the world in a give-and-take fashion—which seems to be required in order for

---

3. Augustine, *The Confessions*, ed. John E. Rotelle, trans. Maria Boulding (Hyde Park, N.Y.: New City Press, 1997), bk. XI, ch. 13.

4. John Owen, *A Practical Exposition upon Psalm CXXX*, in *The Works of John Owen*, ed William Goold (Edinburgh: Banner of Truth Trust), 6:622.

God to be genuinely personal—then He must exist in such a way that allows Him to experience the passage of time. How else could He be affected by temporal creatures, and how else could His responses to their actions make any sense? Thus, God must be temporal in some respect in order to create and to act in the world in a meaningful, personal sense. This view has been growing in popularity among evangelicals over the past few decades. Not all theistic mutualists are agreed on how to characterize this alleged divine temporality, but all tend to agree that creation is the linchpin that requires temporality in God. If creation is not eternal, then it would seem obvious that God is not eternally Creator of heaven and earth. Therefore, God must have *become* Creator after previously having not been such. This conviction is plainly expressed in the words of Thomas F. Torrance: "While God was always Father and was Father independently of what he has created, as Creator he acted in a way that he had not done before, in bringing about absolutely new events—this means that the creation of the world out of nothing is something *new even for God*. God was always Father, but he *became* Creator."[5] And if God can become Creator, then surely He can become and change in other aspects of His being as well. Isaak Dorner long ago declared that "with the acceptance of a noneternal creation God is posited as mutable."[6] Establishing this possibility of becoming in God is necessary for any mutualist understanding of the God-world relation.

It is my aim in this chapter to argue that the traditional doctrine of eternity requires one to confess God as the eternal Creator of the world and that in fact this confession is a necessary piece of maintaining classical Christian theism as a whole. I will first set forth the basic features of the classical (atemporal) doctrine of eternity. What exactly did Christians of old—and especially the Reformed fathers and scholastics—believe about divine eternity? Second, I will examine some

---

5. Thomas F. Torrance, *The Christian Doctrine of God, One Being Three Persons* (Edinburgh: T&T Clark, 1996), 208.

6. Dorner, *Divine Immutability*, 143. Dorner presupposes that a noneternal world of creatures necessarily results in the affirmation of noneternal creatorhood in God; thus, God must be changeable in order to become the Creator He now is.

recent temporalist approaches that dissent from the traditional doctrine of eternity. Finally, I will set forth the traditional argument that being the Creator is not something God became, but what He eternally is. If this is correct, then the main incentive toward some form of divine temporalism will have been removed, and one of the major underlying foundations of theistic mutualism will have been eliminated.

Fundamentals of the Classical Doctrine of Eternity

In order to better understand precisely what is involved in confessing God to be timelessly eternal, we will consider in turn the meaning of divine eternity, the traditional interpretation of the Bible's passages on eternity, and a few other supporting doctrines that explain why God's eternity must be timeless rather than merely an endlessly extended successive duration.

Meaning of Divine Eternity

The basic claim of the classical doctrine of eternity is that God does not experience successive states of being and thus has no future and no past. Positively, eternity is derived from the belief that God is so perfect and infinite in being that no new state of being can come upon Him, and neither can any state of being slip away from Him. He is purely and infinitely actual in all that He is.[7] Boethius, a philosopher and theologian in the sixth century, memorably describes God's eternity as "the whole, simultaneous and perfect possession of boundless life."[8] A bounded life, by contrast, is one that comes into one's possession little by little and that which is also liable to pass out of one's possession. The Boethian formula has been reproduced since the sixth

---

7. For a brief and careful summary of the claims of the classical doctrine of eternity, see Edmund Runggaldier, "Divine Eternity as Timeless Perfection," *European Journal for Philosophy of Religion* 8 (Summer 2016): 169–82. For a more extended philosophical defense of the classical view, see Paul Helm, *Eternal God: A Study of God without Time*, 2nd ed. (Oxford: Oxford University Press, 2010).

8. Boethius, *Philosophiae Consolationis*, V, 6 [10–11], in *The Theological Tractates/The Consolation of Philosophy*, trans. H. F. Stewart, E. K. Rand, and S. J. Tester (Cambridge, Mass.: Harvard University Press, 1973).

century by countless theologians. The Reformed theologian Francis Turretin carefully unfolds its meaning:

> True eternity has been defined by the Scholastics to be "the inter-minable possession of life—complete, perfect, and at once." Thus it excludes succession no less than end and ought to be conceived as a standing, but not a flowing, now. The reason is because noth-ing flows away with time from the life of God as from ours. God has every moment at once whatever we have dividedly by suc-cession of time. Hence philosophers have well said that neither the future nor the past (he will be or was), but only the present (he is) can properly be applied to him. For the eternal duration of God embraces indeed all time—the past, present and future; but nothing in him can be past or future because his life remains always the same and immutable.[9]

Geerhardus Vos, the father of modern Reformed biblical theology, echoes this same sentiment when he defines eternity as "that attribute of God whereby He is exalted above all limitations of time and all suc-cession of time, and in a single indivisible present possesses the content of his life perfectly (and as such is the cause of time)."[10]

That which is perfect and indivisible in being cannot be subject to change, mutation, or movement. It cannot acquire or lose any actuality of being. But all temporal succession involves change from one state of being to another. Turretin thus writes, "For he is not always the same for whom almost every moment something anteriorly is removed and by whom posteriorly something is added." He adds, "The succession and flow of the parts of duration (which exist successively) neces-sarily involve a certain species of motion (which cannot be applied to God)."[11] Successive duration, or *time*, is the measure of a thing's

---

9. Turretin, *Institutes of Elenctic Theology*, vol. 1, III.10.6.

10. Geerhardus Vos, *Theology Proper*, vol. 1 of *Reformed Dogmatics*, trans. and ed. Richard B. Gaffin Jr. (Bellingham, Wash.: Lexham Press, 2014), 10.

11. Turretin, *Institutes of Elenctic Theology*, vol. 1, III.10.3. It should be clear that when Turretin elsewhere speaks of God's "eternal duration," he is using "duration" in an improper and accommodated sense. Properly understood, duration denotes a thing's successive manner of existence.

movement from state of being *A* to a different state of being *B*. Eternity, then, is the negation of these three ingredients of all temporality: (1) a term *from* which (*terminus a quo*); (2) a term *to* which (*terminus ad quem*); and (3) the measure of movement between them.[12] This does not mean that God cannot measure the movements of His creatures, but it does require that He Himself is not moved in measuring them. His knowledge of change does not involve a change of knowledge in Himself. Stephen Charnock states, "All other things pass from one state to another; from their original to their eclipse and destruction; but God possesses his being in one indivisible point, having neither beginning, end, nor middle."[13] Such are the basic claims of the classical doctrine of eternity.

Interpreting Scripture's Passages on Eternity

One challenge facing the traditional understanding of God's eternity as timelessness is that the biblical references to eternity do not in themselves make it clear whether eternity is atemporal or merely an unending succession of moments. Numerous passages speak of eternity in terms agreeable to the latter. Still others speak of God as exalted above and before all time, as if He stood beyond chronology altogether. How can God be described by temporal terms and yet exist beyond all temporality?

First, Scripture applies the language of eternity in an improper fashion to many things that are not eternal in the strict sense. It speaks, for instance, of the following: an eternal covenant (Gen. 17:7); an eternal possession of land (Gen. 17:8); eternal Mosaic rites, ceremonies,

---

12. This is a standard denial in the classical Christian tradition. Aquinas expresses this common outlook when he explains, "Eternity is known from two sources: first, because what is eternal is interminable—that is, has no beginning nor end (that is, no term either way); secondly, because eternity has no succession, being simultaneously whole." *Summa theologiae* Ia.10.4.

13. Charnock, *Existence and Attributes*, 1:284. Edward Leigh defines eternity and time in this same vein: "Eternity is a being without limitation of time, or a being without beginning, ending, or succession. Time is the continuance of things past, present and to come, all time hath a beginning, a vicissitude, and an end, or may have, but God's essence is bounded by none of these hedges." *A Systeme or Body of Divinity* (London: William Lee, 1662), 176.

and promises (Num. 10:8; 15:15; 18:8, 11, 19, 23); eternal moun-
tains (Gen. 49:26; Deut. 33:15); Solomon's temple on Mount Zion as
God's eternal dwelling place (1 Kings 8:13; 9:3; Ps. 132:14); the earth
as immovable forever and ever (Ps. 104:5); eternal life given to God's
elect (John 10:28; Titus 1:2); an eternal weight of glory presently
being produced in believers (2 Cor. 4:17); and an eternal, heavenly
home awaiting God's people (2 Cor. 5:1). Each of these realities has
a temporal beginning and proceeds through a succession of moments.
Some have already passed away and will never return. Others will pass
away at the end of this present age. Still others will go on endlessly
into the future. Francis Turretin observes that eternalist language is
used for these various temporal realities because by "their long continuance and constant duration they seem to approach eternity." Moreover,
eternalist language "may be used for that which has no end, although
it might have had a beginning, as the angels and souls are eternal."[14]
These things are more enduring and stable than other temporal things
and thus seem to imitate more closely the unchanging eternity of God.
Eternity is a comparative term in these instances, denoting those temporal things that are more permanent than others. Inasmuch as God's
eternity is an entailment of His absolute immutability, eternalist terms
are employed in an imprecise way to describe temporal things that are
relatively and comparatively less mutable than other temporal things.[15]

Second, while Scripture uses eternalist language to describe temporal things, it also employs temporalist imagery to speak of God's
eternity. He is called the *Ancient* of Days (Dan. 7:9, 22). It is said that
His *years* have no end (Ps. 102:27). His eternity is said to be "from
the day" (Isa. 43:13). He is *before* the created world, *from* everlasting
to everlasting (Ps. 90:2). Are these expressions to be taken in a strictly

14. Turretin, *Institutes of Elenctic Theology*, vol. 1, III.10.2. See also Gill, *Body of
Divinity*, 45.

15. Thomas uses the term "aeviternal" to characterize those created things that
seem to more closely approximate eternity. This is still not strict eternality in the atemporal sense. Even so, the relative lack of change in certain creatures—such as angels and
the souls of humans enjoying the beatific vision—gives them a manner of existence
that seems to be situated somewhere between eternity and time (as it is experienced by
material beings on our earth). See *Summa theologiae* Ia.10.5.

literal sense? Is God ancient so as to be thought of as very old? Is His life parceled out by years and days? Is His existence chronologically prior to that of the world, and does God advance *from* one state of everlastingness *to* another? The classical interpretation of such expressions regards them as analogies or metaphors meant to accommodate man's inescapable temporal standpoint. Wilhelmus à Brakel explains,

> Even when years or days, or past and present times are attributed to God, and He is called the Ancient of Days and other similar expressions, such is merely done from man's viewpoint. The reason for this is that we, insignificant human beings incapable of thinking and speaking about eternity in a fitting manner, may by way of comparison—which in reality is a very unequal comparison—comprehend as much of eternity as is needful for us to know. Nevertheless, in doing so we must fully divorce God from the concept of time.[16]

Girolamo Zanchius says something similar: "We being in time cannot understand those things that in God are eternal, but after a manner of things temporal, and such words as signify time."[17] In other words, Scripture accommodates itself to the human manner of speaking and thinking, which is entirely temporal.

Third, it is not only the temporal names and descriptions that are given to God that might seem to suggest some temporality in Him but also the unfolding of His effects in time. Because the works of God in history follow successively one after another, we might imagine that God Himself is going through some sequence as the agent producing these works. Yet the traditional view on eternity insists that the succession is only in the things produced and not in God as the agent. There is no succession of activity in God. Turretin maintains, "When the actions of God are considered as either past or present or future this is said not with respect to the efficient reason, but in

---

16. à Brakel, *Christian's Reasonable Service*, 1:92.

17. Girolamo Zanchius, *Life Everlasting*, ed. Robert Hill (Cambridge: John Legat, 1601), 9. Spelling has been updated. See also Aquinas, *Summa theologiae* Ia.10.1, ad 4: "As God, although incorporeal, is named in Scripture metaphorically by corporeal names, so eternity though simultaneously whole, is called by names implying time and succession."

reference to the effects and objects (which are produced in diverse times and on which his acts are terminated)."[18] To sustain this position will require the consideration of a few other supporting doctrines.

Dogmatic Motivations for the Doctrine of Eternity

In order to ensure that eternity is not merely a different sort of *successive* existence that precedes time—an uncreated time that is chronologically prior to created time, so to speak—we must consider the demands of a few other classical doctrines. In particular, the doctrines of divine infinity, immutability, and simplicity lend strong support to the claim that God's eternity is nonsuccessive in character.

Infinity

Biblical texts commonly used to establish God's infinity are those that deny limitations to His being or declare Him to be immeasurable or unfathomable (e.g., 1 Kings 8:27; Job 11:7–9; Ps. 145:3). Infinity is also founded upon the understanding of God's perfection as that to which no higher degree of perfection can be added. Because of this, He is without limitation. Edward Leigh defines divine infinity as "that whereby God cannot be limited, measured, or determined of anything, being the first cause from whom, and the end whereby all things are made." Thus, God is "free altogether from all limitation of time, place, or degrees."[19] Time, as the measure of movement between states of being, is only properly spoken of with reference to finite beings. Herman Bavinck explains this in a dense but important passage:

> Intrinsic time is the mode of existence by virtue of which things have a past, present, and future as so many parts which, whatever the standard employed, can be measured and counted. Now whatever can be measured and counted is subject to measure and number and thus limited, for there always remains a measure and

---

18. Turretin, *Institutes of Elenctic Theology*, vol. 1, III.10.15. By "efficient reason" Turretin means the intrinsic activity of God Himself as the agent who brings about changes in time. In short, God's intrinsic act of agency by which He produces effects is timeless, but this timeless agency finds its terminus in temporal effects.

19. Leigh, *Systeme or Body of Divinity*, 170.

a number greater than that which was measured and numbered. Accordingly, the essential nature of time is not that either with respect to the earlier or the later it is finite or endless, but that it encompasses a succession of moments, that there is in it a period that is past, a period that is present, and a period that comes later. But from this it follows that time—intrinsic time—is the mode of existence that is characteristic of all created and finite beings.[20]

Making his point even more sharply, Bavinck insists, "One who says 'time' says motion, change, measurability, computability, limitation, finiteness, creature."[21]

Immutability

Aquinas notes the inextricable connection between divine immutability and eternity, writing, "The idea of eternity follows immutability, as the idea of time follows movement.... Hence, as God is supremely immutable, it supremely belongs to Him to be eternal."[22] Wilhelmus à Brakel echoes Aquinas, noting, "God unchangeably exists while time is in progression."[23] If time is indeed the numbering of change or motion, then it should be clear why an immutable God cannot be temporal. He cannot undergo change from an anterior state of being to a subsequent state of being, because that would both remove and add actuality of being to His existence (even if not to His essence, as modern-day temporalists are keen to remind us).

Simplicity

Timeless eternity also follows from the doctrine of divine simplicity and its denial that God is composed of parts.[24] If God should be in time, then the full actuality of His life would be built up out of temporal parts—that is, of really distinct before-and-after moments.

---

20. Bavinck, *Reformed Dogmatics*, 2:162–63. See also Aquinas, *Summa theologiae* Ia.10.4.

21. Bavinck, *Reformed Dogmatics*, 2:163.

22. Aquinas, *Summa theologiae* Ia.10.2.

23. à Brakel, *Christian's Reasonable Service*, 1:92. Gill observes that eternity and immutability "infer one another." *Body of Divinity*, 48.

24. This doctrine is discussed at greater length in chapters 3 and 4.

Temporal beings must necessarily exhibit a variety of existential states since time is the measure of movement between these states. These various existential states, not being identical with each other, are really so many parts of the temporal being's complete existence and life. But if God is without parts, then there can be no movement between the parts and thus no *measure* of the movement between the parts. Hence, God is timeless. As à Brakel observes, "There can be no chronology within the Being of God since his Being is simple and immutable."[25] Plainly put, in a simple God there can be no real distinction between before and after. Thus, there can be no temporality, no meditating movement between anterior and posterior states of being. It is no wonder that à Brakel, following the implications of simplicity, insists, "God's being is eternity and eternity is God's being."[26]

Contemporary Dissent from the Classical Doctrine of Eternity

The classical doctrine of eternity is organically related to a host of other doctrines about God that are traditionally confessed by orthodox Christians. But theistic mutualists believe that the notion of divine timelessness locks God out of any meaningful interaction with the world. For this reason, many evangelicals, including a number of modern Calvinists, have undertaken to replace, modify, or augment the classical doctrine of eternity so as to make room for some giveand-take interaction between God and the world. I will survey three of these different approaches, devoting the lion's share of attention to those theistic mutualists who fall within the Calvinist camp.

Temporal God

The first position that should be noted is of those who deny the timelessness of God altogether and instead insist that God's eternity simply means that He perpetually passes through an endless succession of moments. Nicholas Wolterstorff, a leading advocate of this viewpoint, prefers to characterize God as "everlasting" as opposed to eternal. He is concerned that if we do not say God acts as a historical

---

25. à Brakel, *Christian's Reasonable Service*, 1:92. See also Gill, *Body of Divinity*, 48.
26. à Brakel, *Christian's Reasonable Service*, 1:92.

agent (a time-bound actor), then we falsify the Bible's clear testimony to His redemptive actions on behalf of sinners. He argues, "If we are to accept this [biblical] picture of God as acting for the renewal of human life, we must conceive of him as everlasting rather than eternal. God the Redeemer cannot be a God eternal. This is so because God the Redeemer is a God who *changes.* Any being which changes is a being among whose states there is temporal succession."[27]

Wolterstorff's concern is straightforward. Some things God does in history follow after other things He does. Therefore, because there is a sequence of divine effects, there must be something about the divine actor Himself that allows Him to begin to do what He previously did not do and to cease doing what He once did. Surely God does not speak to Moses from the burning bush at the same moment in time as He parts the Red Sea. The latter follows after the former. Wolterstorff asks, "And does not this sort of succession constitute a change on God's time-strand—not a change in his 'essence,' but nonetheless a change on his time-strand?"[28] He concludes that if God begins to do what He previously did not do, then it must be that His "life and existence is itself temporal."[29]

Timeless-Turned-Temporal God

Other theologians agree with the temporal God argument—that, in order to cause any new thing or event, God must exist as a temporal being. But, in distinction from the strong temporalist position of Wolterstorff, they argue that prior to creation God existed timelessly. William Lane Craig is the leading advocate of this position. If God existed before time and creation—as Craig believes the Bible indicates in passages such as Proverbs 8:22–23, 2 Timothy 1:9, Titus 1:2–3, and Jude 25—then it must be the case that God was once timeless

27. Nicholas Wolterstorff, "God Everlasting," in *God and the Good: Essays in Honor of Henry Stob*, ed. Clifton J. Orlebeke and Lewis B. Smedes (Grand Rapids: Eerdmans, 1975), reprinted in Brian Davies, ed., *Philosophy of Religion: A Guide and Anthology* (Oxford: Oxford University Press, 2000), 485.

28. Wolterstorff, "God Everlasting," 495.

29. Wolterstorff, "God Everlasting," 503.

in some respect.[30] On the other hand, once God creates the world, He seems to enter new relations as Creator and Sustainer, and it is difficult to imagine that He could exist in such relations without being touched by the temporality of the world itself. Craig explains this motive for affirming divine temporality: "By virtue of his creating a temporal world, God comes into a relation with the world the moment it springs into being. Thus even if it is not the case that God is temporal prior to his creation of the world, he undergoes an extrinsic change at the moment of creation which draws him into time in virtue of his real relation to the world."[31]

We can see the theistic mutualist supposition at work here. If God creates, then He is drawn into a give-and-take relationship with creation. Craig finds convincing arguments on both sides of the temporalist and eternalist debate. Yet he does not believe both could be true of God at once. It must be the case, he concludes, that God's eternity gave way to temporality at the moment of creation. He states his basic claim quite simply: "With the creation of the universe, time began, and God entered into time at the moment of creation in virtue of his real relations with the created order. It follows therefore that God must be timeless without the universe and temporal with the universe."[32]

Timeless-and-Temporal God

Another mixed temporalist position agrees with much of the timeless-turned-temporal view, except that its advocates do not believe God forfeited His timeless eternity in creating the world. They are desirous to uphold a true confession of God's atemporal eternity. Even so, they

---

30. William Lane Craig, "Timelessness and Omnitemporality," in *God and Time: Four Views*, ed. Gregory E. Ganssle (Downers Grove, Ill.: IVP Academic, 2001) 131–32.

31. Craig, "Timelessness and Omnitemporality," 141.

32. Craig, "Timelessness and Omnitemporality," 156. Craig is aware that his view appears to require that there are two phases of God's life, a timeless and a temporal, with the timeless phase being chronologically earlier than the temporal. But, oddly, he denies that this is what his view actually amounts to inasmuch as describing the timeless phase as "earlier than" the temporal phase ascribes a temporal designation to timelessness itself, which is logically incoherent. Many scholars find Craig's denial on this point to be wholly incongruous with his view that God was once timeless but now is not.

maintain that God's relation to the world as Creator and Redeemer seems to demand that God must exist and act temporally in some respect. Therefore, His eternity needs to be augmented by some measure of temporality. Rob Lister advances this view, arguing that there are "certain divine attributes and...certain dispositions of passion that God takes on in respect to his creation."[33] These are attributes or states of being that God assumes in addition to His essence for the purpose of relating Himself to creatures in time. Temporality of action is a key ingredient in this package of new divine attributes. Lister writes, "I would maintain that part of God's accommodation of himself to us is his taking on the property of acting in time."[34] This is not something God possesses *as the eternal God*. Indeed, Lister draws a sharp distinction between God's "pre-creational timelessness" and His "temporal participation with us, following creation."[35] God's temporality does not displace His essential timelessness but supplements it, so to speak, in order to allow God to create and interact with His creatures in time. Although God's sovereign plan for creation and redemption is eternal, God's "unfolding experience of it occurs in the temporally progressive covenantal context."[36] The demands of theistic mutualism loom large in this explanation of God's newly procured attributes, particularly the demand that God participate in time with His creatures.

John Frame also proposes a model of God as timeless and temporal. Like Lister, Frame believes that in bringing about His sovereign plan, God must ontologically enter the vicissitudes of time as covenantally present to it. Frame explains:

A covenantally present God, like a temporalist God, can know (and assert) temporally indexed expressions like "the sun is rising now." He can feel with human beings the flow of time from

---

33. Lister, *God Is Impassible and Impassioned*, 225.

34. Lister, *God Is Impassible and Impassioned*, 231.

35. Lister, *God Is Impassible and Impassioned*, 228–29. Virtually the same argument is offered by Ware, "Modified Calvinist Doctrine of God," 86–89.

36. Lister, *God Is Impassible and Impassioned*, 230. One detects reverberations of Dorner's view in Lister's remarks. Dorner maintains that "what in his decree is eternally present to God in idea, he himself experiences historically only with the world." *Divine Immutability*, 152.

one moment to the next. He can react to events in a significant sense.... He can mourn one moment and rejoice the next. He can hear and respond to prayer in time. Since God dwells in time, therefore, there is give-and-take between him and human beings.... So God is temporal after all, but not merely temporal. He really exists in time, but he also transcends time in such a way as to exist outside it. He is both inside and outside the temporal box—a box that can neither confine him nor keep him out.[37]

How does Frame hold together divine timelessness and temporality? It is tempting to regard his notion of "temporal omnipresence" as a state of being that supplants God's immutability and timelessness, much like Craig maintains. Yet Frame resolutely maintains that "God is unchangeable in his atemporal or supratemporal existence."[38]

The key to Frame's doctrine is his apparent belief that God's existence extends beyond his atemporality. As Creator and providential Lord of time, Frame believes that God also exists as a changing being within history itself. He can say this because he believes that "there are two modes of existence in God."[39] Frame does not agree that biblical talk about change in God is merely anthropomorphic, as the classical view explained it. Rather, if God acts in time, then He really exists temporally. Frame writes:

History involves constant change, and so, as an agent in history, God himself changes. On Monday he wants a certain thing to happen, and on Tuesday he wants something else to happen. He is grieved one day and pleased the next. In my view, this is more than just anthropomorphic description. In these accounts, God is not merely *like* an agent in time; he really is *in* time, changing as others change. And we should not say that his atemporal, changeless existence is more real than his changing existence in time, as the term *anthropomorphic* might suggest. Both are real.[40]

---

37. Frame, *Doctrine of God*, 558–59.
38. Frame, *Doctrine of God*, 570.
39. Frame, *Doctrine of God*, 572.
40. Frame, *Doctrine of God*, 571.

Frame ascribes two existences to God—one timeless and immutable and the other temporal and changeable.[41] The latter is a new existential manner of being that Frame believes God assumed at creation. "The difference between God's atemporal and historical existences begins," he explains, "not with the creation of man, but with creation itself."[42] God's act of creating is where Frame locates the origin of His temporality. This conviction that God is a temporal creator is indispensable to the theistic mutualist insistence on a God who can, in Frame's words, "feel with human beings" and "react to events in a significant sense." For Frame, the foundation for God's ontological becoming and experiences of change in history is laid in His alleged first experience of becoming and change at creation.

Another proponent of the timeless-and-temporal doctrine is K. Scott Oliphint. Creation appears to serve as a key motivator for his ascription of ontological newness to God. Oliphint states, "God freely determined to take on attributes, characteristics, and properties that he did not have, and would not have, without creation. In taking on these characteristics, we understand as well that whatever characteristics or attributes he takes on, they cannot be of the essence of who he is, nor can they be necessary to his essential identity as God."[43]

Oliphint proposes a model very similar to Lister's and Frame's, though he utilizes the hypostatic union of the divine and human natures in Christ as an explanatory key for understanding how God can be both eternal and temporal.[44] Just as the Son is eternal according to His divine nature and temporal according to His human nature,

---

41. This duality of being is also a key component of Dorner's revisionist project. The similarity between his viewpoint and Frame's is noteworthy: "To be sure, he is in himself always wholly and immutably the same. But his being for the world and in it is something different." *Divine Immutability*, 153.

42. Frame, *Doctrine of God*, 571.

43. Oliphint, *God with Us*, 110.

44. The recent evangelical penchant for finding in Christology the key to the mysteries of theology proper and the God-world relation is also proleptically set forth in Dorner's strategy. "Christology," he writes, "presents the archetype, the utterly perfect form of union between God and humanity in general. The way in which the uniting of the divine and human is conceived in Christology is at the same time decisive and typical for a series of other dogmas." Thus, according to Dorner, "the objective fundamental

so Oliphint insists God is eternal in His essential character and temporal in His covenantal character. God, he writes, "takes on temporal properties without in any way ceasing to be essentially eternal."[45] For Oliphint, as for Frame and Lister, the fact of creation and God's action therein is the occasion for attributing new nonessential being to God: "The fact that God interacts at all with creation presupposes his covenantal character. Once he determines to relate himself to us, that relation entails that he take on properties that he otherwise would not have had. He limits himself while remaining the infinite God. The fact that he is Creator means that he is now related to something *ad extra* to which he was not related before."[46]

On Oliphint's account, creatorhood is a new and thus temporal property in God that is really distinct from what God is as essentially infinite and eternal. By "covenantal character," Oliphint means a mode of being God has taken on in addition to His divine essence in order to interact with creatures. He believes that it is only by assuming the temporal "covenantal property" of Creator that God can create or act in time. What sets Oliphint's view apart from Frame's and Lister's is that, given his incarnational explanatory template, he seems to conceive of God's assumed temporal properties as creaturely properties rather than new divine properties.[47]

---

fact of Christianity, the incarnation of God, is the factual solution to the problem of the uniting of God's immutability and vitality." *Divine Immutability*, 160, 164.

45. Oliphint, *God with Us*, 13n8. Bruce Ware similarly appeals to the incarnation of the Son as a model for explaining how God takes on temporality in addition to His essential atemporality. "Modified Calvinist Doctrine of God," 89.

46. Oliphint, *God with Us*, 188.

47. For Oliphint, God's covenantal relation to His creation requires an ontological reality for God that is distinct from His divinity. Oliphint explains that God "remains who he is, but he decides to be something else as well; he decides to be the God of the covenant." *God with Us*, 254. It is clear that Oliphint believes Creator is part of the "something else" that God begins to be. See *God with Us*, 16–17. This reality for God is new, he claims, something "which had not been the case before." *God with Us*, 255. On this account it would seem that Creator is not properly a *divine* reality inasmuch as nothing truly divine can begin to be. Also, if the incarnation of the Son is the model, and if the "covenantal properties" are analogous to the humanity the Son assumed, then it turns out that the "covenantal properties" cannot be divine since the humanity of the Son is not divine. If this were not the case, then it becomes unclear exactly how

Summary Assessment

What can we say in response to the various temporalist views? We must first observe the common conviction that binds them together: *God cannot create or bring about temporal effects without ontologically participating in the temporality of His creation.* Whatever their disagreements may be regarding the notion of divine timelessness—never timeless, no longer timeless, or presently timeless and temporal—all are agreed on at least this one thing, which thinking proceeds thus: A temporal effect can only proceed from a temporal act of causation, and such acts can only go forth from temporal agents. Thus, God cannot act in the temporal realm without somehow existing on the same temporal ontological continuum with His creatures. Creation, accordingly, is not merely something that goes forth from God, but it is also an action that God begins to perform at some point in time. It thereby denotes a real change of activity in Him by requiring that He pass from a state of inactivity to activity, of not-creating to creating. When God acts to create or produce changes in the world, He Himself is moved or changed in the process by becoming the actor He previously was not. On this account, God becomes Creator. Negatively expressed, the basic conviction is that God cannot be present to time *in His eternity*. Timelessness seems to lock Him out of the world. It is a barrier to any action or relation to the world on God's part. This is deeply at odds with the classical doctrine of eternity, as we shall see.

It is fitting at this juncture to say something with respect to the widespread tendency to deny that God changes essentially while allowing that He does undergo change in other aspects of His being. There

---

the incarnation is supposed to explain God's assumption of new attributes. Oliphint's incarnational analogy carries the strange implication that God's "covenantal properties" are a second and created nature, and thus that God *as Creator* is in fact a creature. It is unclear what prevents other creatures from potentially being Creator in the same sense as God is, just as all humans are human in the same sense as the Son is. Paul Helm's critique of Ware on this point is also apropos to Oliphint's argument: "The analogy with the incarnation is not apt, for Christ is two natured, but the immanence of God is not a nature of God alongside his transcendence." "Response by Paul Helm," in *Perspectives on the Doctrine of God: Four Views*, ed. Bruce A. Ware (Nashville: B&H Academic, 2008), 122.

is no inconsistency on the part of Wolterstorff in making such a claim inasmuch as he denies both divine immutability and simplicity. But this strategy of denying essential change while admitting nonessential change in God is not available to those who claim to hold to a classical conception of immutability or divine simplicity. This is because according to the simplicity doctrine there is nothing in God that falls outside of His essence or is really distinct from it. When theologians in the classical tradition deny essential change in God, they mean to deny *all* change in God whatsoever—because there is nothing in Him that is not identical with His essence. Modern evangelicals who offer a model of God as both essentially immutable and nonessentially mutable have effectively abandoned the doctrine of God's simplicity. They presume that there is some accidental actuality in God that exists alongside His essence.

Confessing the Eternal Creator

Nothing that begins to exist can be regarded as properly divine. Divinity has no origin, limit, or measure. This has profound implications for the way we regard God's creatorhood. If being Creator should be something temporal that God becomes, it would seem to follow that His actions in and toward the world *as Creator* are not properly the actions of God *as divine*. A creatorhood that begins to be cannot be regarded as an aspect of God's divinity as such, but, ironically, must be considered as a creaturely property.[48] On the other hand, it does sound odd to say that God is eternally Creator. Eternalists traditionally have been quite willing to endorse the incomprehensible notion that God is immutably and eternally Creator and that God creates the world *as the Eternal One*.[49] How do they account for this strange teaching?

---

48. Réginald Garrigou-Lagrange succinctly states the principle that underlies this judgment: "What is found in a being without properly belonging to it according to its nature, is something which has been caused in it. In fact, not possessing this characteristic of itself and immediately (*per se primo*), it can possess the same only in a conditional manner, by reason of another." *God: His Existence and His Nature*, trans. Dom Bede Rose (St. Louis: B. Herder, 1934), 1:317.

49. For a recent account, see Paul Helm, "Eternal Creation," *Tyndale Bulletin* 45 (1994): 321–38.

Nothing Mediates God's Relationship to the World

First, eternalists deny that God's agency in and toward the world as its Creator, Sustainer, and Redeemer can be divorced from His being or accounted for in terms of something God has become in addition to what He is essentially *as God*. Consider the statement of Herman Bavinck in this connection: "It is God who posits the creature, eternity which posits time, immensity which posits space, being which posits becoming, immutability which posits change. *There is nothing intermediate between these two classes of categories*: a deep chasm separates God's being from that of all creatures."[50] The point is that if God should take on intermediary properties of being by which He acts in the world—such as Lister's "acting in time," or Oliphint's "covenantal properties"—then these properties, which are themselves not God, would form the foundation for God's agency in the order of creation. Plainly put, if God should require the acquisition of new properties in order to mediate His activity toward and in the world, then He could not act in the world *as divine*, as God.[51]

Creator: A Relative Name Denoting an Absolute Reality

Second, classical eternalists tend to distinguish between the manner in which creatures come to *name* God as Creator, and the *reality* of creatorhood in God Himself. God comes to be known and termed by us as Creator through our observation of His created effects in time.

---

50. Bavinck, *Reformed Dogmatics*, 2:158–59. Emphasis mine.

51. Note that properties are commonly understood as ontological foundations for action, those features of a thing's being in virtue of which it acts. For example, a wise man acts wisely in virtue of the wisdom that is in him, and a strong man performs feats of strength in virtue of the property of power in him, and so forth. With respect to God's action, we might similarly say that God acts in virtue of what is in Him. Thus, if creatorhood is not in God eternally, then it must be that He does not act in creation *as eternal*—that is, in virtue of His eternality. He must acquire some property of being in addition to His eternal essence in order to act in the world. This is similar, perhaps, to the way a wise man, who is not wise in virtue of his human essence, must acquire wisdom in addition to his essence in order to act wisely. For those who deny that creatorhood belongs to God in His eternal essence, it must follow that God does not act in the world in virtue of His divine essence but rather in virtue of that which He has come to be in addition to that essence.

But in identifying God's relation of creating through His effects, we are not picking out a newly acquired property of being in God. Zanchius observes, "Those names which argue a relative respect between God and his creatures, as the names Creator, Lord, Redeemer, [and so forth], are indeed in time given to him, and not from eternity, yet so as that no new thing is added to him, neither is there any change in him."[52]

Creator, Lord, and Redeemer are not accidental features of existence that are appended to God's essence. Bavinck writes similarly, "Relative names, such as 'Lord,' 'Creator,' 'Sustainer,' 'Savior' and so on, belong to God only on account of and upon the coming into being of, the creation."[53] Yet Bavinck further explains that all the names assumed by God in virtue of the various ways He relates Himself to creatures "definitively denote something in God that exists in him absolutely."[54] Many Reformed theologians point to Augustine's remarks along these same lines: "Accordingly, that which is first said of God in time, and was not said of him before, is manifestly said of him relatively, yet not because of some accident in God, as though something happened to him, but plainly on account of some accident of that with reference to which God begins to be called something relative."[55]

It is not difficult to stumble on Augustine's and Bavinck's twofold affirmation in this connection. On the one hand, they insist that God is not called Creator from eternity; and on the other, they maintain that this name "Creator" picks out an absolute reality in God and is not something He began to be. What are we to make of this? It is perhaps helpful to understand the difference between the twin affirmations — that "Creator" is a relative name and denotes an absolute reality — as corresponding to the epistemic-noetic activity of the human knower on the one hand, and the ontological reality of God's absolute being on the other. The difference lies not in a twofold manner of God's existence — timeless and temporal, for example — but in the distinction

52. Zanchius, *Life Everlasting*, 20. Spelling updated.

53. Bavinck, *Reformed Dogmatics*, 2:133–34.

54. Bavinck, *Reformed Dogmatics*, 2:134.

55. Augustine, *De Trinitate*, V, 16, cited in Bavinck, *Reformed Dogmatics*, 2:134. See also Aquinas, *Summa theologiae* Ia.13.7.

between (1) the human manner of knowing and predicating about God and (2) God's actual manner of existing. The coming-to-be and the relativity, so to speak, are in the event and manner of humans naming God "Creator," but not in the being and activity of God Himself.[56]

Creation: An Eternal Act Producing a Temporal Effect
Third, the older tradition taught that creation is an eternal act of God that produces a temporal effect. God's act of creating is eternal. The thing created is temporal. This may seem perplexing, but the reasoning is rather straightforward. The divine act of creation is nothing other than the eternal action of God's immutable will. Thus, there is no distinction in agency between God's will to create and the act of creating (see Rev. 4:11). They are the same act in God. If God's will for the world is eternal, then so is His effective activity as Creator. He does not need to supplement His eternal act of will to create with a distinct and subsequent act of creation. We might contrast this to human acts of production in which the act of producing chronologically follows after and is really distinct from the act of planning to produce—as driving the nails is a distinct and subsequent act to drawing up the blueprints for a house. In God, the willing *is* the producing. The producer and

---

56. Reformed theologians traditionally allowed a distinction between absolute and relative attributes in our God-talk. This distinction was not meant to suggest that some of God's attributes are ontologically relative, but simply that some things we say about God are said only from the standpoint of our relation to God as creatures in time—and thus relatively. Steven Duby distills the basic features of this twofold way of speaking about God:

> The absolute attributes "belong to God from eternity and without respect to creatures," while the relative "belong to God in time with some relation toward creatures." The former are identical to God's essence considered absolutely (though still under diverse aspects), while the latter are identical to God's essence considered in relation to the creature under some aspect of creaturely circumstance. God does not undergo change so as to accrue the relative attributes as accidents; rather, the creature undergoes change, taking up a new relation to God and thus meeting the same divine essence in new ways.

Divine Simplicity, 205. Duby's citations are from Amandus Polanus, *Syntagma Theologiae* (Hanoviae: N.p., 1615), II.32.

His act of production are timelessly eternal; what is produced is temporally indexed and creaturely.[57]

Turretin explains that when the world goes forth from God into being, no "new will enters into him, but only a new external work proceeds from his eternal efficacious and omnipotent will." He further states, "By the same practical volition which he had from eternity, he created the world in time—produced it actually in the beginning of time."[58] The divine act of production is not what begins with time, but only the thing produced. E. L. Mascall observes, "The Christian tradition has consistently maintained that creation is a nontemporal act of the divine will by which the whole temporal created order is maintained in existence, and that the creation and conservation of the

---

57. This is not to suggest that the world is temporal because it chronologically follows after some period of duration that preceded it. The world's absolute beginning in existence is not a moment that succeeds a previous moment. Such an understanding would effectively deny that time begins with creation since the period that precedes creation would be temporally proximate to the world as its chronological predecessor. The world, understood as the totality of the created order, does not chronologically follow after or precede anything. Rather, all succession between before and after is within the world itself. Strictly speaking, creation appears *with* time, not *in* time. See Augustine, *Confessions*, bk. XI, chs. 10–13; and Bavinck, *Reformed Dogmatics*, 2:429: "The world was not made in time but along with time." Inasmuch as creation *ex nihilo* is not a change but rather an absolute coming to be—that is, it involves no motion from some already existing state of being, no *terminus a quo*—it follows that there is no movement for time to measure in creation. For this reason also creation is not in time. On the motionlessness of the world's production in being, see Thomas Aquinas, *Summa contra Gentiles*, bk. 2, ch. 17.

58. Turretin, *Institutes of Elenctic Theology*, vol. 1, III.7.1. Compare Turretin's words to the claims of T. F. Torrance in which Torrance argues that to say God became Creator "is not to say…that God did not always have the power to create, nor is it to say that creation was not in the Mind of God before he actually brought it into being, but that he brought it into being by a definite act of his gracious will." *Christian Doctrine of God*, 208. Torrance regards God's power to create as a capacity for action, as passive potency in need of some principle of act—namely, a definite act of God's will—to move it into actuality. By willing to create he conceives of God as moving His power from bare potential to actuality. This is patently at odds with the demands of divine simplicity, which denies all composition of act and passive potency in God. It further renders God's *actual* power in creation the consequent of a particular act of the divine will. In other words, God makes Himself to be what He was not by new acts of His will.

universe is one timeless act."[59] If this is a true characterization of God's will and act of creating, then creation brings about no change in God.[60]

The question of eternal creation can be needlessly complicated if we fail to distinguish the different ways we use the term "creation." It can be used as a verb of God's act of creating, or as a noun to identify the things created. Edward Leigh observes that some acts of God proceed from His being and terminate upon creatures. When we speak of these acts—such as creation, providence, calling, sanctification, and glorification—we need to distinguish between the act itself in God and the things upon which that act terminates. He argues, "We must distinguish between the action itself, and the work. God's act in Creating is the act of his will, that such a Creature should stand up in time, *Creatio* is but *Essentia Divinis relatione ad Creaturam*, Aquinas. But if we consider *opus*, the work it selfe, so the Creatures have a being one after another."[61] Upholding this profound distinction between God's eternal act (*actus*) of creating and the temporal work (*opus*) created is

---

59. Mascall, *He Who Is*, 62.

60. Etienne Gilson notes the deep mystery of this confession: "It is absolutely true that all movement is a changing of the state of being. But when we hear of an act which is not a movement we are at a loss how to think about it. No matter how we try, we always *imagine* that creation is a kind of change.... But in actual fact it is something quite different, something we are at a loss to put into words, so unfamiliar is it to the conditions of human experience." *The Christian Philosophy of St. Thomas Aquinas*, trans. L. K. Shook (New York: Random House, 1956), 122. Strictly speaking, the Christian doctrine of creation is not a doctrine of becoming so much as it is a doctrine of the coming forth of "the whole of being from the universal principle of being." Te Velde, *Aquinas on God*, 139.

61. Leigh, *Systeme or Body of Divinity*, 177–78. The reference to Aquinas is drawn from his *Summa theologiae* Ia.45.3, ad 1: "Creation signified actively means the divine action, which is God's essence, with a relation to the creature." In an exposition of Aquinas's view, James Anderson observes that "every finite action or operation is an accident and as such it presupposes for its exercise a preexisting subject or matter. Since creative action is not an accident, it is identical with the substance of the agent. But this agent is none other than God." *The Cause of Being: The Philosophy of Creation in St. Thomas* (St. Louis: B. Herder, 1952), 27–28. Rudi te Velde reminds us that if God is simple then the intrinsic act by which He creates is the same as the act by which He exists or is any of the other things we attribute to Him: "It follows from the doctrine of divine simplicity that in God, being, knowing, loving and creating are all identical." *Aquinas on God*, 69.

absolutely crucial if we are to avoiding dragging God down into some manner of time-bound existence and agency.

The implication of all this should be clear. A consistent confession of God's eternity must be fearless in affirming that God is in fact eternal Creator. Herman Bavinck maintains this mystery in a truly striking passage in his *Reformed Dogmatics*:

> On the one hand it is certain that God is the Eternal One: in him there is neither past or future, neither becoming or change. All that he is is eternal: his thought, his will, his decree. Eternal in him is the idea of the world that he thinks and utters in the Son; eternal in him is also the decision to create the world; eternal in him is the will that created the world in time; eternal is also the act of creating as an act of God, an action both internal and immanent. For God did not *become* Creator, so that first for a long time he did not create and then afterward he did create. Rather he is the eternal Creator, and as Creator he was the Eternal One, and as the Eternal One he created. The creation therefore brought about no change in God.[62]

Conclusion

Theistic mutualism claims that God experiences change via His interaction with the world. The belief that God *became* Creator is the foundation for this insistence upon ontological becoming in God. But the assumption that in creating God had to undergo change is by no means obvious, at least not to those who refuse to think of God as a finite causal agent.[63] If God is indeed the eternal Creator that classical

---

62. Bavinck, *Reformed Dogmatics*, 2:429.

63. Consider the remarks of Réginald Garrigou-Lagrange in this regard: "The formal concept of causality does not *per se* include any of those imperfections which are found in finite beings. To say that an action is causal, means that it is a realizing action, but not necessarily accidental, temporal, formally transitory and transitive. These imperfections constitute the created mode of causality, but this notion [of causality], for the sole reason that it denotes an absolute and analogical perfection, is susceptible also of another mode." *God: His Existence and His Nature*, 1:220. Thomas Aquinas reminds us that "eternity excludes the principle of duration, but not the principle of origin." *Summa theologiae* Ia.42.2, ad 2. Just because creaturely acts of origination are always temporal, it does not follow that origination necessarily entails temporality.

Christian theism confessed Him to be, then creation does nothing to motivate or ground theistic mutualism.

Peter Sanlon is surely correct when he writes, "It is all too easy to assume that God experiences time in a manner very similar to us, albeit with greater insight and vision. Even if we accept that God, as creator, must be radically different than his creation, we struggle with temporal words to express this."[64] Yet the strangeness of confessing God to be the eternal Creator must not be allowed to stop us. This is because the alternative of a God who becomes Creator is not merely strange, but positively opposed to God's absoluteness and to our worship of Him. It suggests that God does not act in the world as the God that He is from all eternity, but as something else that He has come to be. But then this something else cannot be divine and so cannot be the proper object of our worship. If God should act in the world as the Creator who He has *come to be*, then we would not adore Him *as divine* when we worship Him as Creator. No less than true religion is at stake in the contest between theistic mutualism and classical Christian theism.

---

64. Sanlon, *Simply God*, 83.

CHAPTER 6

One God, Three Persons

If there should be any aspect of classical Christian theism that would appear to have been left intact by evangelical theistic mutualists, it would seem to be the doctrine of the Trinity. In many respects, this is indeed the case. Evangelical theistic mutualists are avowed monotheists who maintain the real distinctions among the Father, Son, and Holy Spirit in the Godhead. Moreover, they tend to confess the unity of the Godhead in the classically orthodox language of God's oneness of being, substance, and essence.

Nevertheless, theistic mutualists face a difficulty with respect to the Trinity to the extent that they discard the strong classical account of divine simplicity. The fact is that if simplicity and its unique requirements are denied, any number of compositional models of divine unity might adequately explain how the one God subsists as three distinct persons. And it is not apparent that a compositional model of divine unity must *necessarily* be monotheistic rather than tritheistic.[1] Without divine simplicity, the Father, Son, and Holy Spirit potentially could be understood either as three parts of God—in which case each person would ontologically precede the being of God and each would lack something of the fullness of divinity—or as three discrete beings or gods who collectively make up a social unit we call God.

---

1. Scott R. Swain expresses this concern quite candidly. "To put the matter baldly," he writes, "there was and is no need for the doctrine of the Trinity if God is not simple, for there were and are plenty of sophisticated and unsophisticated ways of conceiving how three persons may comprise one complex divine being or community." "Divine Trinity," in *Christian Dogmatics: Reformed Theology for the Church Catholic*, ed. Michael Allen and Scott R. Swain (Grand Rapids: Baker Academic, 2016), 102–3.

The question facing Christians is not merely whether or not we believe that God is one or if the three persons are a divine unity. Rather, the question is at an even deeper level: What *sort* of oneness and unity should we ascribe to God? According to Herman Bavinck, "The oneness of God does not only consist in a unity of singularity… but also in a unity of simplicity."[2] Just any garden-variety unity will not do. Thomas Aquinas notes that all beings are one (i.e., undivided) either by virtue of simplicity or composition. A simple being is one and undivided because it lacks parts and so could not possibly fail to be a unity. A compound being is one and undivided as a result of the composition of all its parts or constituents.[3] Every compound being possesses features that are really distinct from its essence and which combine with the essence to give it particularity. Thus, for instance, we may say that to be human and to be *this* particular human are not one and the same thing. It is this capability of the essence's composition with some additional particularizing features that allows an essence to be instantiated in a series of multiple beings of the same kind. But for a simple being, multiplication in a series is impossible since it is not composed of essence plus some particularizing feature. Rather, everything in the being *just is* identical to the essence. Thus, for God to be God, and for God to be *this* God we call Yahweh and whom we know by the name Father, Son, and Holy Spirit—this is simply just one and the same reality. Without a sufficiently strong doctrine of simplicity, it becomes unclear why the three persons are not three gods (or three parts of the essence that are themselves less than wholly divine) and why the divine unity is not merely a moral and communal unity. It is only because God is simple that all the data concerning the three distinct persons of the Godhead cannot possibly be reimagined in a tritheistic direction.

Lacking recourse to the doctrine of simplicity, it should not be surprising that theistic mutualist explanations of divine unity have moved progressively in the direction of compositional accounts of God's unity, most notably that of social trinitarianism. After all, a

---

2. Bavinck, *Reformed Dogmatics*, 2:173.
3. See Aquinas, *Summa theologiae* Ia.11.1.

compound model of God's unity is all that is available after one abandons divine simplicity. Increasingly, the strategy has been to deploy the classical doctrine of perichoresis (i.e., the mutual indwelling of the divine persons) to account for the unity of the Godhead. In this way, relations rather than unity and identity of substance provide the foundation for God's oneness. The difficulty with this is that the classical tradition generally regards perichoresis itself as an entailment of God's simple and substantial unity. Furthermore, it is not clear why a doctrine of perichoresis untethered from the demands of divine simplicity and substantial unity could not just be an exotic form of tritheism. No doctrine of unity besides the simple unity of identical substance can absolutely guarantee God's exclusiveness or ensure that the fullness of the Godhead is in each person—both claims of which are indispensable to the doctrine of the Trinity.

In this chapter, I will first consider the historic attempt to maintain God's simplicity and singularity through the confession of His substantial unity. I will then look at the basic biblical and theological aspects of divine unity. After that, I will briefly note the real distinctions between the divine persons in the Godhead and introduce the idea of the persons as subsistent relations in God. Finally, I will evaluate various compositional alternatives to God's simple and substantial unity, most notably social trinitarianism.

Historical Confession of Substantial Unity

The doctrine of the Trinity is one of the most perplexing mysteries of the Christian faith.[4] It requires us to affirm many things about God at

---

4. Augustine soberly and piously prefaces his discussion of the Trinity with the following words: "I will be attempting to say things that cannot altogether be said as they are thought by a man—or at least as they are thought by me. In any case, when we think about God the Trinity we are aware that our thoughts are quite inadequate to their object, and incapable of grasping him as he is.... Now since we ought to think about the Lord our God always, and can never think about him as he deserves; since at all times we should be praising him and blessing him, and yet no words of ours are capable of expressing him, I begin by asking him to help me understand and explain what I have in mind and to pardon any blunders I may make. For I am as keenly aware of my weakness as of my willingness." *The Trinity*, bk. 5, 1.

once that seem very difficult to fit together. The doctrine rests on three basic biblical affirmations: (1) there is only one true God; (2) Scripture identifies three who are distinct as God; and (3) these three are coequal and coeternal in their divinity. The Athanasian Creed expresses well the mystery that Scripture compels us to confess, "We venerate one God in the Trinity, and the Trinity in oneness; neither confounding the persons nor dividing the substance.... The divine nature of the Father and of the Son and of the Holy Spirit is one.... Thus the Father is God, the Son is God, and the Holy Spirit is God; and nevertheless they are not three gods, but there is one God."[5]

While this seems suitable for maintaining what Scripture requires us to believe about God, it profoundly challenges our customary ways of thinking. How can one be three—and three, one? The temptation is to soften some aspect of the mystery in order to make it more comprehensible. Historically this has led to any number of heretical outcomes. For instance, if one denies the real distinctions among the three persons, Sabellianism (modalism) results. If one denies that each and every person possesses the fullness of divinity, subordinationism results. And if one divides the substance so as to conceive of divinity as a generic essence with three particular instantiations, tritheism (polytheism) results.

The first major challenge to the doctrine of the Trinity was modalistic Monarchianism or Sabellianism. The second was Arian subordinationism. Tritheism seems not to have been a significant threat during the early centuries of the church.[6] In fact, if one surveys the beliefs of both the orthodox fathers and the early heretics, one of the things they all seem to agree on is that God must be one being.

---

5. *Enchiridion Symbolorum*, 39, in Henry Denzinger, ed., *The Sources of Catholic Dogma*, trans. Roy J. Deferrari (Fritzwilliam, N.H.: Loreto Publications, 2002).

6. In the second century, Marcion's polytheism was roundly repudiated by the church. An outbreak of tritheism occurred in the sixth century as an extension of the monophysite controversy. See G. L. Prestige, *God in Patristic Thought* (London: S.P.C.K., 1952), 273, 282–84. See also John of Damascus's discussion of John Philoponus's tritheistic teaching in *On Heresies*, 83, in *Saint John of Damascus: Writings*, trans. Frederic H. Chase Jr., The Fathers of the Church, vol. 37 (New York: Fathers of the Church, Inc., 1958).

The singular unity of being (or substance) was nonnegotiable.[7] The challenge lay in characterizing this divine oneness in a way that did justice to the full range of biblical data. The Sabellians feared that saying there are three distinct persons who are God would undermine the monarchy of the Godhead, transforming it into an oligarchy and thus implying more than one principle of being back of creation. The Arians also were concerned to safeguard the singularity of God's being or substance. They reasoned that as the begottenness of the Son seems to indicate some beginning of the Son, and since it belongs to the divine substance not to begin to exist, it must be that the Son is of a different and inferior substance to the Father. Indeed, the Son must be the highest creature who began to exist at some point.[8]

The goal of the orthodox trinitarian fathers at Nicaea in AD 325 was to answer the Arian denial of the Son's full divinity. They did so by affirming that the Son is "Light of Light, very God of very God" and is of the "same substance" (homōousia) with the Father. Against the Arians, they avowed the full divinity of the Son, who lacked nothing that belonged to the divine substance of the Father.[9] It is important to note that the substantial unity of the Godhead was affirmed by

---

7. This is not surprising in light of that fact that at the time of the Council of Nicaea "God's transcendent Being, immutable and impassible, eternal and underivative, was an assumption that went unquestioned by all parties." Frances M. Young, *From Nicaea to Chalcedon: A Guide to the Literature and Its Background*, 2nd ed. (Grand Rapids: Baker Academic, 2010), 241.

8. Consider the words of Arius in this regard: "And God, being the cause of all things, is Unbegun and altogether Sole, but the Son being begotten apart from time by the Father, and being created and founded before ages, was not before His generation.... For He is not eternal or coeternal or co-unoriginate with the Father, nor has He His being together with the Father, as some speak of relations, introducing two ingenerate beginnings, but God is before all things as being Monad and Beginning of all." Arius to Alexander of Alexandria, cited in Athanasius, *De Synodis*, part 2, ch. 16, in *Nicene and Post-Nicene Fathers*, vol. 4.

9. Among Arius's sympathizers there were those (notably, the Eusebian party) who were concerned that the language of homōousia might result in the full identification of the Son with the Father, which was the error of the Sabellians. It would not be until later in the fourth century when theologians would make a clear conceptual distinction between the terms *ousia* (substance) and *hypostasis* (person).

all the parties involved in those early controversies.[10] G. L. Prestige observes that "the long history of the evolution of Trinitarian doctrine is the record...of orthodox insistence on the true and full deity of the three Persons historically revealed, as against the attempts of heresy to maintain the doctrine of divine unity by misconceived and mischievous short-circuits."[11]

There are many ways to confess that God is one, though most of them turn out to be incompatible with the full range of biblical revelation concerning God. This is clearly the case with modalism and Arianism in their respective failures to acknowledge real distinctions among the divine persons or the full divinity of each of the three. But this would also be the case if one were to confess the real distinction among the persons together with their coequality of divinity and yet fail to explicate their oneness in such a way as to ensure it is not a *composite* unity. Such would threaten true monotheism by undermining divine simplicity. The pro-Nicene fathers attempted to uphold a noncomposite unity of the three persons by ascribing to them an identity of substance.[12] This approach was consistently upheld throughout the medieval period and in many of the Protestant confessions of the sixteenth and seventeenth centuries. The Second London Confession of Faith's article on the Trinity (2.3), for instance, sits squarely with the pro-Nicene fathers and medieval schoolmen:

---

10. While the term *homoousion* would come to be understood as signifying numeric identity of substance among the persons of the Godhead, divine unity per se was not the main concern of the Nicene fathers. Prestige notes, "As far as the Council of Nicaea is concerned, the problem of the divine unity did not arise. The question it had to settle was whether both the Father and the Son were God in exactly the same sense of the word God." *God in Patristic Thought*, 213. Without qualification, *homoousion* could potentially signify the same kind of generic substance or stuff common to several individuals of a class. The monotheistic elaboration of the term as an indicator of divine unity fell to the subsequent defenders of Nicaea, most notably Athanasius. Indeed, as Prestige observes, "The employment of homoousios by Athanasius to express substantial identity was a new development in Greek language." *God in Patristic Thought*, 219.

11. Prestige, *God in Patristic Thought*, 300.

12. In contrast to the theistic mutualist understanding of the divine essence as a composite essence comprised of various attributes (see the discussion in chapter 4), the pro-Nicene fathers would have regarded the divine substance as a truly simple unity.

In this divine and infinite Being there are three subsistences, the Father, the Word or Son, and Holy Spirit, of one substance, power, and eternity, each having the whole divine essence, yet the essence undivided: the Father is of none, neither begotten nor proceeding; the Son is eternally begotten of the Father; the Holy Spirit proceeding from the Father and the Son; all infinite, without beginning, therefore but one God, who is not to be divided in nature and being, but distinguished by several peculiar relative properties and personal relations; which doctrine of the Trinity is the foundation of all our communion with God, and comfortable dependence on Him.[13]

We should note in particular the "one substance" of the Father, Son, and Holy Spirit and the fact that God is "not to be divided in nature and being." In these expressions, any hint of tritheism is eradicated from the classical doctrine of the Trinity. If one supposes that the unity of substance is a generic unity so that the persons are particular instances of divinity—as some have suggested is compatible with Nicene trinitarianism[14]—the denial of nature-being composition rules out such a possibility. The being of the persons is not really distinct from that of the divine nature, and thus the persons cannot relate to the essence as species to a genus or as individuals to a species. In this way, the monotheistic credentials of Christian trinitarianism are preserved against any possibility of tritheism. To understand what motivates such a nuanced interpretation of divine unity, we will briefly consider the basic features of the classical approach to God's unity of being.

Unity of Divine Being

Herman Bavinck notes that God's unity of singularity means "that there is but one divine being, that in virtue of the nature of that being God cannot be more than one being and, consequently, that all other beings

---

13. Dennison, *Reformed Confessions*, 4:536.

14. Gijsbert van den Brink, for instance, believes that the orthodox formula of "three *hypostaseis* in one *ousia*" allows for "generic accounts of the divine unity." See "Social Trinitarianism: A Discussion of Some Recent Theological Criticisms," *International Journal of Systematic Theology* 16 (July 2014): 341.

exist only from him, through him, and to him."[15] The Second London Confession begins its chapter "Of God and of the Holy Trinity" with the affirmation that "the Lord our God is but one only living and true God."[16] This monotheistic conviction is rooted both in the biblical witness of the Old and New Testaments and in the conviction that the ultimate cause of all being must be infinite and so exclusive in existence.[17]

Biblical Witness to God's Exclusivity

We find abundant witness to God's singularity and exclusivity in the Old Testament. Deuteronomy 6:4 famously declares, "Hear, O Israel: The LORD our God, the LORD is one!" This is the ontological basis for the exclusive and unreserved worship that He demands from humans (Deut. 6:5). God will tolerate no other gods before Him (Ex. 20:3), and indeed besides Him there are no other gods (Deut. 4:35; 32:39). David asks in Psalm 18:31, "For who is God, except the LORD?" His mighty act of creation distinguishes Him as the true God over against all imposters. Psalm 96:5 states, "For all the gods of the peoples are idols, but the LORD made the heavens." To Isaiah, God says, "Before Me there was no God formed, nor shall there be after Me" (Isa. 43:10). He adds, "Indeed before the day was, I am He" (v. 13). And in well-known words He declares, "I am the First and I am the Last; besides Me there is no God" (Isa. 44:6).

In the New Testament, this same affirmation of God's exclusivity persists. It is significant that the revelation of God's threefold personal

---

15. Bavinck, *Reformed Dogmatics*, 2:170. The peculiar feature of God's nature that ensures He "cannot be more than one being" is His simplicity.

16. Dennison, *Reformed Confessions*, 4:535.

17. Stephen Holmes argues that social trinitarianism tends to isolate the New Testament witness to divine threeness while downplaying the more comprehensive witness of Holy Scripture to the oneness of God: "One cannot claim a position is 'biblical' without considering the whole of scripture, not just the New Testament. The totality of the biblical witness concerning God...consists of a sustained and pointed witness to the oneness of God in the face of repeated temptations to polytheisms, supplemented by a brief coda or appendix suggesting that this One God is in fact triune." "Three Versus One? Some Problems of Social Trinitarianism," *Journal of Reformed Theology* 3 (2009): 86–87.

subsistence, most clearly disclosed in the redemptive missions of the Son and Spirit, does not soften the early church's monotheistic convictions. In John 17:3, Jesus prays to the Father and calls Him "the only true God." He also indicates that He had glory together with the Father before the world existed in verse 5. This is remarkable considering Isaiah 42:8, in which God declares that He will not give His glory to another. We can only conclude that the Son Himself is the only true God, even as the Father. In Romans 3:30, Paul declares that the God who justifies both the circumcised and uncircumcised is one. And in 1 Corinthians 8:4, Paul says that we know there is no such thing as an idol in the world and that there is no God but one. Strikingly, in the context he proceeds to identify this one God as the Father and Son: "For even if there are so-called gods, whether in heaven or on earth (as there are many gods and many lords), yet for us there is one God, the Father, of whom are all things, and we for Him; and one Lord Jesus Christ, through whom are all things, and through whom we live" (vv. 5–6).[18] Paul is not contrasting the Father and Son but rather the Father and Son, who are one God, to the pretend gods, which are the idols. Paul's ascription of creation to both Father and Son is significant in that "Creator" can be said only of the one who is true God (cf. Acts 17:24–28; Rom. 11:36). In 1 Timothy 2:5, Paul again states, "For there is one God." James 2:19 tells us that we do well to believe God is one. These New Testament affirmations of God's singularity are as exclusivist as those in the Old Testament. The mystery is that these affirmations of divine unity clearly include distinct persons.[19] How are we to hold the truth of monotheism together with the fact that three distinct persons are identified as this one true God?[20]

---

18. The last phrase of verse 6 is probably better rendered "though whom we exist" or "through whom we are."

19. For a helpful discussion of the biblical witness to God's singularity, see Duby, *Divine Simplicity*, 91–108.

20. The Son is clearly identified as God in a number of passages. John 1:1–4, the Word was with God, was God, and made all things; John 8:58, Jesus calls Himself "I AM"; John 20:28, Christ is called "God" by Thomas; Romans 9:5, He is called "God blessed forever"; Philippians 2:6, Christ Jesus exists "in the form of God" (μορφῇ θεοῦ, "form" arguably denoting essence or substantial form); Titus 2:13, Paul confesses

Divine Nature

If we are to identify the Father, Son, and Holy Spirit as the one God of whom Scripture testifies, we must first ask what it is they have in common that warrants such identification. What makes each person God? The short answer to this question is that each is possessed of the exact same nature. Broadly speaking, a thing's nature is what distinguishes it from all other kinds of beings and thus provides its quiddity (or what-ness). More narrowly, a thing's nature is what serves as the foundation for its activity. The Bible itself employs nature language to refer to God's Godness. Romans 1:20 speaks of God's "Godhead" or "divine nature" (θειότης) that is clearly seen through what has been made. This is to suggest that there is something that we call "divinity" by which God is divine and which is the foundation for His act of creation—the Godness of God, so to speak. Colossians 2:9 uses the same sort of terminology when it informs us that the fullness of the Godhead or deity (τὸ πλήρωμα τῆς θεότητος) dwells in the Son—the fullness of God's nature or Godness. Paul uses the term "nature" when he speaks in Galatians 4:8 of those idols to which Christians were formerly enslaved as "by nature...not gods" (φύσει μὴ οὖσιν θεοῖς). The clear implication is that the God who freed us from our sins and idolatry is God *by nature*. This nature is what makes God to be God, as it were.

Him as "our great God and Savior Jesus Christ"; Colossians 1:15–17, Christ is the image of the invisible God and all things are created by, through, and for Him (cf. Rom. 11:36); Hebrews 1:3, Christ is the radiance of God's glory and the exact representation of His nature, the one who upholds all things by the word of His power; John 1:18, He is the "only begotten Son who is in the bosom of the Father." These passages are only a sampling of the clear New Testament witness to the Son's identity as God. The New Testament also identifies the Spirit as God: Acts 5:3–4, to lie to the Spirit is to lie to God; 1 Corinthians 2:10–11, the Spirit knows the thoughts of God perfectly (cf. Ps. 147:5); 2 Peter 1:21, the Spirit is the one who inspires the Word of God. Moreover, He grants to us all the benefits of salvation acquired by Christ: He convicts the world of sin (John 16:8–11); grants us the status of children of God (Rom. 8:14–16); regenerates and renews us (Titus 3:5); pours out God's love in our hearts (Rom. 5:5); produces spiritual fruit in us (Gal. 5:22–23); seals our salvation to us (Rom. 8:23; 2 Cor. 1:22; 5:5); and grants to us new life in raising us up with Christ (Rom. 8:10–11; cf. Eph. 2:4–6). Only one who is God can save sinners and give new life from the dead.

Unity of Simplicity

Yet orthodox Christians do more than confess that the three divine persons are possessed of a common nature. They also confess that each person is the exact *same* God. How do we know that this nature is unique to one divine being? After all, the fact that humans possess a common human nature—the same human essence or substantial form of humanity—does not entail that there is only one human. Why would the common possession of the divine nature, or essence, entail that the three divine persons are one and the same God? Why not three gods? Surely that would seem more straightforward. Besides the clear biblical testimony to God's singular exclusivity, which bars us from confessing a plurality of gods, the answer lies in the consequences of divine simplicity.[21]

In a multitude of beings of the same kind or class there is something more in the being of the individual than just the nature or essence by which it is defined. That is, something more than the nature or essence as such gives it distinction from all others in the class. This distinctive quality may be one's particular matter or perhaps some other accidental features of its being. But in God, there can be nothing that He is that lies outside His nature—no determination of His being in addition to His essence. If there were, God would require something beyond His divinity, His Godness, for the fullness of His being. For

---

21. The Bible's various claims to God's exclusivity, if understood in isolation from the implications of divine simplicity, do not appear sufficient in themselves to prove monotheism beyond the shadow of a doubt. This is because without the requirements of simplicity, it is possible, even if improbable, that the passages recording God's declarations of His singular exclusivity are merely the statements of a corporate entity comprised of really distinct beings. There is biblical precedent for corporate entities comprised of really distinct beings making claims to exclusivity and even deploying first-person singular pronouns to do so. Babylon, for instance, idolatrously misappropriates the divine name, saying, "I am, and there is no one else besides me" (Isa. 47:8, 10; cf. Zeph. 2:15). How do we know that God's many claims to exclusivity are not spoken in a similar manner—to wit, as the claims of a single corporation comprised of really distinct beings? Something more than the claims to exclusivity alone seems to be needed to show that monotheism is absolutely necessary and not just one possible interpretation of the data. For this reason the classical Christian creeds and confessions frequently couple the avowal of God's singularity with the affirmation of His simplicity.

God to be divine and for God to be *this* God we call Yahweh are one and the same reality. Thus, divinity cannot be a genus or species in which divine persons exist as so many particular instantiations. Those who maintain the classical doctrine of simplicity deny that there is any distinction in God between suppositum and nature. God has no real particularizing features over and above His divine nature. This feature of simplicity rules out any possibility that true divinity could appear in a plurality of beings really distinct from each other, for instance, as true humanity (nature/essence) is able to appear in a plurality of really distinct humans (supposita).[22] It is thus divine simplicity that undergirds monotheism and ensures that it does not just so happen that God is one, but it must be that God cannot but be one being because of what it means to be God.[23]

---

22. In *Summa theologiae* Ia.11.3, Thomas appeals to this feature of the simplicity doctrine as his first reason for confessing the oneness of God:

> It is manifest that the reason why any singular thing is 'this particular thing' is because it cannot be communicated to many: since that whereby Socrates is a man, can be communicated to many; whereas, what makes him this particular man [Socrates], is only communicable to one. Therefore, if Socrates were a man by what makes him to be this particular man, as there cannot be many Socrates, so there could not in that way be many men. Now this belongs to God alone; for God Himself is His own nature.... Therefore, in the very same way God is God, and He is this God. Impossible is it therefore that many Gods should exist.

See also the discussion in Aquinas, *Summa theologiae* Ia.3.3; à Brakel, *Christian's Reasonable Service*, 1:98–99; Dolezal, *God without Parts*, 52–55. See also te Velde, *Aquinas on God*, 84: "There can be but one single God, because what it means to be God—utterly simple and most perfect—excludes the possibility of multiplication and division. It is therefore impossible that there should be many Gods."

23. To the demands of simplicity we should also add the demands of divine infinity. Gill makes the argument that an infinite must be exclusive in being. "To suppose two infinites," he explains, "the one must either reach unto, comprehend, and include the other, or not; if it does not, then it is not infinite, and so not God; if it does reach unto, comprehend, and include the other, then that which is comprehended, and included by it, is finite, and so not God; therefore it is clear that there cannot be more infinites than one; and if but one infinite, then but one God." *Body of Divinity*, 127. Thomas makes this argument in *Summa theologiae* Ia.11.3. He further explains that divine simplicity is a necessary condition for divine infinity in his remarks in *Summa theologiae* Ia.7.1: "Since therefore the divine being is not a being received in anything, but He is His own

Unity of Substance

When classical theists confess that the Father, Son, and Spirit are "one substance, power, and eternity," they mean they are one and the same being.[24] As each person has the complete divine essence, we confess that each is God unqualifiedly. The essence is not divided among them. No one person possesses a feature of divinity that the other two lack, nor is the whole of divinity greater than what is possessed by each person—as humanity as such is greater than any individual man, for instance. If there is any suggestion that the unity of divine substance is a generic unity, this is explicitly ruled out by the insistence that God is not to be divided in nature and being. Whatever is in God is ontologically identical to His divine nature. To be Father, Son, and Holy Spirit is not something that God is over and above His divine essence. The persons do not add being to God beyond the divine nature, and the divine nature is not something more than what is in each person. Divinity itself is identical to the Father, Son, and Holy Spirit. The

---

subsistent being as was shown above (Question 3, Article 4 [demonstrating that God is not composed of essence and existence]), it is clear that God Himself is infinite and perfect." That is, God's existence is not bounded by His essence, being identical with it, and is therefore without limitation.

24. Aristotle distinguished between primary and secondary substance in creatures. The primary is the concrete substance itself; the secondary is that abstract or generic substantial form (or essence) by which the thing is what it is. This cannot apply to God since the concrete God is not merely a particular instantiation of a generic divine essence. In every such instantiation, there is some real distinction between the essence as such and the features that particularize the concrete individual. The *divine* essence just is the concrete God. Richard Muller explains the position of the Reformed orthodox on this matter:

> Since God is one, sole, and absolute, and since there is but a single undivided divine essence or substance, there can be no genus "god." There is no divine "essence" apart from the one, individual divine "substance." The distinction between primary and secondary *ousia* does not apply: understanding "god" as indicating a secondary essence is characteristic of polytheism, where an essence is shared by various divine beings. Therefore, the terms "substance" and "essence" are roughly equivalent in their application to God: the individual being (substance) of God is inseparable from the identity or whatness (essence) that God is.

PRRD, 4:173.

Puritan William Ames makes clear that we do not maintain a generic unity among the persons, declaring, "He is said to be one not in kind, but in that perfect unity which is often called numerical and individual in creatures."[25]

Although this seems to be the only way to ensure that the Father, Son, and Holy Spirit are each the numerically same God, it undoubtedly leaves us with many questions. What is a divine person? Can divine persons be really distinct from each other? And if they are really distinct from each other, how can they be identical with the divine essence without somehow reducing the essence to some sort of complexity or composition? Indeed, what is the relation between the divine essence and the persons? Each of these questions deserves much more consideration than can be afforded to it in the scope of this present survey.[26] Nevertheless, a few remarks concerning personal distinctions in the Godhead are fitting at this juncture.

Real Distinction among Divine Persons

The following remarks are by no means an explanation but only a brief attempt to show how orthodox Christians have traditionally endeavored to uphold the real unity of substance and distinction of persons in the Godhead. G. L. Prestige writes, "If Christianity is true, the same stuff or substance of deity in the concrete has three distinct presentations—not just three mutually defective aspects presented from separate points of view…but three complete presentations of the whole and identical object, namely God, which are nevertheless objectively distinct from one another."[27]

---

25. William Ames, *The Marrow of Theology*, trans. John Dykstra Eusden (Boston: Pilgrim Press, 1968), 86.

26. For a more detailed discussion, see James E. Dolezal, "Trinity, Simplicity and the Status of God's Personal Relations," *International Journal of Systematic Theology* 16 (January 2014): 79–98; Thomas Joseph White, "Divine Simplicity and the Holy Trinity," *International Journal of Systematic Theology* 18 (January 2016): 66–93; and Dennis W. Jowers, "The Inconceivability of Subordination within a Simple God," in *The New Evangelical Subordinationism? Perspectives on the Equality of God the Father and God the Son*, ed. Dennis W. Jowers and H. Wayne House (Eugene, Ore.: Pickwick Publications, 2012), 375–410.

27. Prestige, *God in Patristic Thought*, 168.

The Father is not the Son or Spirit. The Son is not the Father or Spirit. And the Spirit is not the Father or Son. Yet these are the one same divine being. What can this possibly mean? We must first note that classical trinitarians insist that the real distinction is not between the persons and the divine essence, but only among the persons themselves. The one God just is the Father, Son, and Holy Spirit. If the persons were really distinct from the essence, which would be the case if any person failed to possess the whole divine essence, then we would be left with a quaternity: Father, Son, Spirit, and essence. We would also be unable to say unreservedly that the Father is God, the Son is God, and the Spirit is God. This outcome is biblically and theologically unacceptable.

Yet the three persons are really distinct. How so? Classical Christian theists generally locate this distinction in personal relations or, in slightly more imprecise language, "several peculiar relative properties." Specifically, it is in relations that we locate the real distinctions of paternity (unique to the Father), filiation or begottenness (unique to the Son), and spirated procession (unique to the Spirit). William Ames expounds the relations in the Godhead by which each person is distinguished from the other two: "The relative property of the Father is to beget.... Hence [the Father is] first in order.... The relative property of the Son is to be begotten, that is, so to proceed from the Father as to be a participant of the same essence and carry on the Father's nature. Hence he is second in order.... The property of the Holy Spirit is to be breathed, to be sent forth and proceed from both the Father and the Son."[28]

---

28. Ames, *Marrow of Theology*, 88. These various relations are the way the one divine nature is communicated in God. Edward Leigh explains:

> The personal property of the Father is to beget, that is, not to multiply his substance by production, but to communicate his substance to the Sonne. The Sonne is said to be begotten, that is, to have the whole substance from the Father by communication. The holy Ghost is said to proceed, or to be breathed forth, to receive his substance by proceeding from the Father and the Sonne joyntly, in regard of which he is called The Spirit of the Father, and the Spirit of the Sonne both, Gal. 4:6. The Father only begetteth, the

How do we know these three are really distinct? Perhaps one might suppose that the distinction is only in the external manifestation of God, not in God Himself, as the doctrine of simplicity claims for the various divine attributes. The reason classic trinitarians do not conclude such a real identity of the persons with one another in God is because it belongs to the proper meaning (or *ratio*) of relation to denote one in reference to another.[29] Otherness or "opposition," as the older theologians would have put it, is proper and strictly irreducible in any relation.[30] None of the essential attributes of God is a relation, properly speaking, and so there is no reason to insist on their "opposition" or real distinction as we do among the three persons of God.[31]

So what are the persons? If they are not three gods or three distinct beings or substances, what can we say about them? Traditionally, many have claimed that the persons are nothing but the relations (paternity, filiation, procession) subsisting in the Godhead. Thomas

---

Sonne only is begotten, and the holy Ghost onely proceedeth; both procession and generation are ineffable.

Systeme or Body of Divinity, 254.

29. Thomas observes that "relation in its own proper meaning signifies only what refers to another." *Summa theologiae* Ia.28.1. His point is that inherence in a subject is not included in the proper *ratio* of a relation, unlike the other eight genera of Aristotelian accidents.

30. Gilles Emery explains the importance of opposition for ensuring the real distinction among the divine persons: "The word 'opposition' obviously does not indicate competition, but must be taken in its formal meaning: opposition is the *principle of a distinction*. This opposition is required because the distinction of the divine persons is not 'material.' No opposition, no distinction: to reject such 'opposition' comes down to an acceptance of Sabellianism." *The Trinitarian Theology of Saint Thomas Aquinas*, trans. Francesca Aran Murphy (Oxford: Oxford University Press, 2007), 98.

31. Some critics of the doctrine of simplicity, such as R. T. Mullins, mistakenly believe divine simplicity means there are "no real distinctions in the simple God" and that "God has no distinctions." For Mullins, simplicity is thus obviously at odds with any affirmation of a real distinction among the divine persons. *The End of the Timeless God* (Oxford: Oxford University Press, 2016), 184. But divine simplicity does not deny distinctions in the Godhead—not even real distinctions—but only such distinctions as would entail composition and so undermine God's pure actuality. See Muller, *PRRD*, 3:57. See also John Owen, *Vindicae Evangelicae*, in *Works*, 12:71: "Those who affirm God to be a simple act do only deny him to be compounded of divers principles and assert him to be always actually in being, existence and intent operation."

Aquinas, tracing out the implications of divine simplicity, writes, "For personal properties are the same as the persons because the abstract and the concrete are the same in God; since they are the subsisting persons themselves, as paternity is the Father Himself, and filiation is the Son, and procession is the Holy Ghost."[32]

This is no doubt a strange way to think of a person. If we consider creaturely persons, we find that each person is also a complete substance really distinct in being from all other persons. Further, in human persons relations inhere as accidents—they don't subsist as persons themselves. Though this is true of creatures, however, it is not true of God.[33] William Ames, tracking Aquinas, speaks representatively of the Reformed orthodox tradition when he states, "A relative property in God implies a person, but this is not so in creatures."[34] Louis Berkhof also spotlights the difficulty of our talk about divine persons: "God is one in his essential being, but in this one being there are three persons,

---

32. Aquinas, *Summa theologiae* Ia.40.1, ad 1.

33. Thomas and the Reformed orthodox insist on identifying the divine persons as *subsisting* relations. If the persons possessed their relations as *inhering* relations (which would be accidents since accidents always appear in a thing's being by virtue of inherence in the thing), then the persons as persons would be really distinct in virtue of something other than their relations. That is, there would be three really distinct persons underlying and more ontologically basic than the relations. The Father would be conceived as a person who *has* paternity, the Son a person who *has* filiation, and the Spirit a person who *has* procession. Persons would precede the relations in being and already exist with a distinction of some sort. It thus would not be the "opposition" contained in the *ratio* of relation that accounted for their real otherness, and we would be forced to find some other basis for alterity among the persons. But all other bases for otherness would seem to be either (1) substantial or (2) accidental. Either way divine simplicity would be undone, and, if substantial differences were the basis for otherness, so would monotheism itself. Insomuch as the proper *ratio* of relation does not include inherence or accidentality and relations cannot be conceived as substances, the idea of "subsistent relations" seems to be the one theologically suitable way for describing what the persons of the Godhead are and how they are really distinct in God. This alone will hold classical orthodoxy together, even if rendering it highly enigmatic.

34. Ames, *Marrow of Theology*, 88. Richard Muller explains further: "The orthodox follow the traditional definition of 'subsistences' in the Godhead as real relations or relative properties, modes of the divine being—which, in the Godhead, can be called persons, as distinct from usages applicable to the creaturely order, where relative properties or real relations in a being cannot be understood as 'persons.'" *PRRD*, 4:184.

called, Father, Son, and Holy Spirit. These persons are not, however, like so many persons among men three entirely separate and distinct individuals. They are rather three modes or forms in which the divine essence exists."[35] Augustine notes the difficulty of person language with respect to God as well: "Yet when you ask 'Three what?' human speech labors under a great dearth of words. So we say three persons, not in order to say that precisely, but in order not to be reduced to silence."[36] The three persons are not complete individual substances inasmuch as that would transform monotheism into a single *class* or *category* of divine being, comprised of multiple gods. This violates the fundamental demands of divine simplicity. When we say "God is one," we mean one concrete and substantive being, akin to Aristotle's notion of primary substance—not one class or genus of being.

What, then, are we saying about God when we speak of the Father, Son, and Holy Spirit? First, it should be observed that we are not speaking of things that are distinct from the Godhead itself. Whenever we speak of the three, we are in fact speaking of the one, but under different aspects or modes of being. We alternatively speak of the one God Father-wise, Son-wise, and Spirit-wise—in sum, relation-wise. These relations are not something really distinct from the divine substance. As John Owen puts it, "A divine person is nothing but *the divine essence... subsisting in an especial manner.*"[37] The challenge is that in our creaturely experience our talk about substances and our talk about relations must necessarily be distinguished. When we speak of what belongs to humans *as human*, we speak of them according to substance. When we speak of them as a parent, child, friend, employee, and so forth, we speak according to relation. Because these two realities—substance and relation—are not strictly identical in the human subject, we speak of

---

35. Louis Berkhof, *Manual of Christian Doctrine* (Grand Rapids: Eerdmans, 1933), 75.

36. Augustine, *The Trinity*, bk. 5, ch. 2, 10.

37. John Owen, *A Brief Vindication and Declaration of the Doctrine of the Trinity*, in *The Works of John Owen*, ed. William Goold (1850–1853; repr., Edinburgh: The Banner of Truth Trust), 2:407.

them as really distinct features of the human's being. Indeed, we have no other speech pattern available to us.

But in God, relations are not features of His being that exist over and above His substance. They add nothing to the substance. They are not principles of actuality adjoined to the divine essence that determine it to exist in some sense, as if the essence were something abstract that is then made concrete in the persons. In God, there is no mixture of abstract and concrete. We are forced to speak of God's essence under the rubric of substance terminology and relation terminology, which Augustine calls "substance-wise" and "relationship-wise."[38] Our inability to say or even think both at once is why we must proceed in this double way of speaking of the one God.[39] Yet this double way of speaking of God, alternatively according to substance and relation, is not to be understood to mirror a double way of being within Himself. He is not composed of substance and relations as creatures are. It is this commitment to divine simplicity that makes the Trinity such a profound mystery. Gilles Emery declares, "Simplicity lays itself down as a fundamental rule of Trinitarian doctrine: God is his own essence or nature, and the persons themselves are this nature."[40]

Compositional Models of Trinitarian Unity

An account of God's oneness as a composite unity would almost surely render the Trinity less enigmatic. Theologians are drawn to less mysterious accounts of the Trinity for various reasons. Some simply refuse to believe in a God that cannot be univocally understood. Univocists believe that language must refer to God in precisely the way

---

38. Augustine, *The Trinity*, bk. 5, ch. 1, 8.

39. Gilles Emery calls this duality in our talk about God's persons "redoublement." It contains two aspects, "the divinity or the divine essence *common* to the three persons, and the *properties* that distinguish the persons." *Trinity in Aquinas* (Ypsilanti, Mich.: Sapientia Press, 2003), 133. See also Levering, *Scripture and Metaphysics*, 214–16.

40. Emery, *Trinitarian Theology of Saint Thomas Aquinas*, 143. See also Aquinas, *Summa theologiae* Ia.3.3 and Ia.39.1. Timothy Smith is surely correct when he maintains that "the incomprehensibility of the Trinity is due to the absolute simplicity of the divine nature." *Thomas Aquinas' Trinitarian Theology: A Study in Theological Method* (Washington, D.C.: Catholic University of America Press, 2003), 123.

it refers to creatures, or it means nothing. Some desire to make the doctrine of the Trinity more practical by envisioning it as a blueprint for human relations and society,[41] and this social practicality would surely be obscured if one were to apply the logic of divine simplicity to the account of God's tripersonal existence. Still others aim to use the doctrine to resolve the philosophical problem of the one and the many, thereby implicitly rendering the unity of the persons a generic unity. While there are diverse motives for making the doctrine of the Trinity more comprehensible, the one thing that seems to bind most recent theistic mutualist accounts together is the replacement of God's simple unity with some version of composite unity.

The compositional model that has enjoyed the widest support in recent decades is social trinitarianism. Not all theologians who endorse a compositional model of God's unity identify themselves as social trinitarians. And some versions of social trinitarianism are rather extreme inasmuch as they explicitly deny substantial unity, characterize the persons as parts of God, or attribute diverse essences to Father, Son, and Holy Spirit. Most evangelical theistic mutualists reject such extreme proposals. It thus seems fitting to distinguish the stronger compositional accounts of social trinitarianism from weaker accounts of compositional unity. I will consider each in turn.

Social Trinitarian Accounts of Compositional Unity

Possibly the most influential advocate of social trinitarianism in recent decades has been the Reformed theologian Jürgen Moltmann. He is concerned that the older trinitarianism that conceives the three persons as three distinct manners of subsistence of the one divine substance erects an unacceptable God-behind-God scenario and is too near to the Sabellian heresy.[42] He prefers instead to conceive the

---

41. Gijsbert van den Brink suggests that it would be "embarrassing" to believers and unbelievers alike if the relevance of the Trinity for ordering our lives in community were questioned. He speaks of the time before the twentieth-century awakening of social trinitarianism as "the ages of trinitarian oblivion and confusion." See "Social Trinitarianism," 339, 350.

42. Jürgen Moltmann writes, "If the subjectivity of acting and receiving is transferred from the three divine Persons to the one divine subject, then the three Persons

unity of the Godhead as the product of the perichoretic fellowship of the three persons. Perichoresis is the ancient teaching that argues that each of the three persons indwells and is interior to the others. Such is reflected in Jesus's words in John 14:11, "I am in the Father and the Father in Me." Each person has its distinct identity and being wholly in relation to the other two. Moltmann wants to say that this network of relations *just is* the unity of the Godhead. "In respect of the Trinity's inner life," he writes, "the three Persons themselves form their unity, by virtue of their relation to one another and in the eternal perichoresis of their love."[43] He claims that this alone is a genuine trinitarian unity and is much to be preferred to the alleged monadic unity proffered by the classical Augustinian insistence on substantial identity.

Among evangelical theistic mutualists, J. P. Moreland and William Lane Craig endorse a form of social trinitarianism. They understand the one divine nature to be an aggregate of the three persons, who themselves are said to be "distinct centers of consciousness, each with its proper intellect and will."[44] They strongly object to the Thomist and Reformed orthodox understanding of the persons as relations, declaring that "on no reasonable understanding of *person* can a person be equated with a relation. Relations do not cause things, know truths or love people in the way the Bible says God does."[45] So how do Moreland and Craig understand the persons in relation to the Godhead? Is the whole divine essence undividedly and properly in each person? They do not believe so. Rather, they maintain that "it is the Trinity as a whole that is properly God." By this they mean that "the Trinity alone is God and that the Father, Son, and Holy Spirit, while divine, are not Gods."[46] Moreland and Craig are loath to affirm with the Athanasian

---

are bound to be degraded to modes of being, or modes of subsistence, of the one identical subject. But viewed theologically this is a late triumph for the Sabellian modalism which the early church condemned. The result would be to transfer the subjectivity of action to a deity concealed 'behind' the three Persons." *The Trinity and the Kingdom: The Doctrine of God*, trans. Margaret Kohl (San Francisco: Harper & Row, 1981), 139.

43. Moltmann, *Trinity and the Kingdom*, 177.

44. Moreland and Craig, *Philosophical Foundations*, 583.

45. Moreland and Craig, *Philosophical Foundations*, 586.

46. Moreland and Craig, *Philosophical Foundations*, 589.

Creed that the Father is God, the Son is God, and the Spirit is God inasmuch as they take "God" to be a reference only to the three as an aggregate whole. So how do we say the persons are divine if no person is possessed of the whole divine substance? Their proposal is that the persons are "parts" of the one God: "We could think of the persons of the Trinity as divine because they are parts of the Trinity, that is, parts of God.... It seems undeniable that there is some part-whole relation obtaining between the persons of the Trinity and the entire Godhead."[47] This denial that the whole divine nature is in each divine person would be similar to calling one's hand, foot, or nose "human," since each is a part of the individual human, while denying that the entirety of humanity is in any one part.

One also finds a proclivity for social trinitarianism among some recent Calvinist theologians. Cornelius Plantinga Jr., for instance, is concerned that the Augustinian tradition's assertion that God has a singular mind, will, love, and action—each of these being aspects of the one simple divine substance—eclipses the true personhood of the Father, Son, and Spirit. Like Moreland and Craig, he understands the three persons "as distinct centers of knowledge, will, love, and action." According to Plantinga, it is only in such distinction that the Father, Son, and Spirit appear "as *persons* in some full sense of that term."[48] Plantinga further insists that any accompanying theory of divine simplicity must be "modest" enough to fit this distinction of consciousness. In other words, a doctrine of simplicity that emphasizes the harmony of knowledge among the three persons is to be preferred over one that holds to an identity of knowledge among them. But Plantinga is still keen to insist on the singularity of God. "Father, Son, and Spirit," he explains, "must be regarded as tightly enough related to each so as to render plausible the judgment that they constitute *a particular social unit.*" He adds, "In such social monotheism, it will be appropriate to use the designator *God* to refer to the whole Trinity, where the Trinity

---

47. Moreland and Craig, *Philosophical Foundations*, 591.

48. Cornelius Plantinga Jr., "Social Trinity and Tritheism," in Oliver D. Crisp, ed., *A Reader in Contemporary Philosophical Theology* (London: T&T Clark, 2009), 68.

is understood to be one thing, even if it is a complex thing consisting of persons, essences, and relations."[49]

Response to Social Trinitarianism

What are we to make of social trinitarianism? It either says too much or too little. On the one hand, it says too much when each person is conceived as having a distinct essence and will of its own. One wonders how this is not the identification of three distinct beings or primary substances. On the other hand, it says too little when it denies that any particular person is possessed of the entire divine essence, the one divine substance. This denies something proper to God's "Godness" to each person. It also appears to make the unity of the Godhead dependent on more basic units of being for its own fullness of being—namely, the individual persons, who constitute the divine being as parts constitute a whole. This undermines divine absoluteness by requiring us to look back of the Godhead itself to some more primitive foundation of being.[50]

With regard to Plantinga's proposal in particular, it should be noted that conceiving of divine unity as a "particular social unit" does not appear at all well suited to the maintenance of monotheism. A baseball team is a particular social unit. So is an incorporated municipality. So is a particular church. Plantinga repeatedly states that the divine persons share a "generic" divine essence. But, aware that this suggests "mere common membership in a class," he further specifies that it is more than mere joint class membership that binds them together. Rather, he argues, they are "also members of the same family."[51] It is not clear why Plantinga thinks this is any better. Families are likewise a sort of class or species and can be comprised of members who are

---

49. Plantinga, "Social Trinity and Tritheism," 68. First emphasis mine.

50. Bavinck observes that the simplicity of God is not "inconsistent with the doctrine of the Trinity, for the term 'simple' is not used here as an antonym of 'twofold' or 'threefold' but of 'composite.'" Thus, he continues, "The divine being is not composed of three persons, nor is each person composed of the being and personal attributes of that person, but the one uncompounded (simple) being exists in three persons." *Reformed Dogmatics*, 2:177.

51. Plantinga, "Social Trinity and Tritheism," 73.

ontologically distinct from each other as individual beings. In other words, in his attempt to say the Father, Son, and Spirit are persons in the "full sense of that term"—whether conceived as particular individuals within a genus or members of the same family—Plantinga's social trinitarianism has removed the safeguards against tritheism. His softening of the demands of divine simplicity plays a key role in this move toward a compositional model of divine unity.

It can also be objected that, contrary to its stated intent, social trinitarianism seems to produce an impersonal deity. By relocating all "personal" traits such as knowing, willing, and loving to the persons, it yields the very God-behind-God it claims to dislike in the older doctrine of substantial unity. Rather than the divine essence or substance lying behind the persons, which is the alleged liability of the classical Augustinian view, it is now the persons who appear to lie behind the divine essence. The essence *as such* is no longer what accounts for divine knowing, willing, and loving. Inasmuch as the essence is where the oneness of God is located, it appears that God *as one* is no longer a personal being—at least not any more personal than a class or corporation might be.[52] Its personal character lies behind its unity rather than in it. The divine substance in the hands of social trinitarians is no longer a singular personal being—a "he" or a "him"—but rather a mere impersonal genus, corporation, or family.

Moreover, appeals to perichoretic unity alone will not suffice to explain why God is one God inasmuch as classically speaking perichoretic unity itself follows from substantial unity. John Owen explains that the "mutual in-being of the persons" is "by reason of their unity in the same substance or essence."[53] Thomas Aquinas offers the same reason for coinherence among the persons: "The Father is in the Son by

---

52. Duby makes a striking observation of the problems involved in such a move: "For God as one is bereft of his knowing, willing, loving, and acting, and what funds the unity of the persons becomes an enigmatic and impersonal deity. Indeed, the reassignment and tripling of these attributes to the three persons entails that the question of *quis* [who] in theology proper is simply not applicable to God as one." *Divine Simplicity*, 220. Duby is specifically responding to Moltmann's proposal.

53. Owen, *Brief Vindication and Declaration of the Doctrine of the Trinity*, in *Works*, 2:408.

His essence, forasmuch as the Father is His own essence, and communicates His essence to the Son not by any change on His part. Hence it follows that as the Father's essence is in the Son, the Father Himself is in the Son; likewise, since the Son is His own essence, it follows that He Himself is in the Father in Whom is His essence…. And the same applies to the Holy Ghost."[54]

It is the communication of substantial unity from the Father to the Son and from the Father and Son to the Spirit that makes the persons one being, not the relations *qua* relations. Matthew Levering writes, "The truth of the Trinity hinges upon the fact that the Father's divine being and unity is eternally shared or communicated, *rather than constituted*, in the 'tripersonal movement of gift.'"[55] The relatedness of the divine persons is what communicates divine unity, not what constitutes it. Accordingly, Duby notes that "perichoresis is actually just an implicate of the identity of the essence in each of the persons."[56] The reason the Father, Son, and Spirit are so perfectly "in" each other is because they are the one same substantial being. Indeed, a perichoretic unity of mutual indwelling shorn of any connection to divine simplicity and substantial identity as its ground cannot *necessarily* prevent one from reconceiving the one God as one intimately related organization of beings or primary substances collectively called "God." Gavin Ortlund argues this point quite lucidly:

> Strictly on the grounds of interpenetration, we are left further to explain why the interpenetration of the Father, the Son and the Spirit does not entail three interpenetrating gods. Why should the interpenetration of three persons yield one undivided unity, and not some complex aggregate? What is needed is not simply a mechanism by which to bring the divine persons into

---

54. Aquinas, *Summa theologiae* Ia.42.5. Prestige observes that while the formal articulation of the doctrine of the coinherence of divine persons (perichoresis, circumincessio) first appeared in the sixth century work of pseudo-Cyril, "it is really involved in the doctrine of the identity of the divine ousia as expressed in each Person," which had been clearly articulated in the fourth century. *God in Patristic Thought*, 284.

55. Matthew Levering, *Engaging the Doctrine of the Holy Spirit: Love and Gift in the Trinity and the Church* (Grand Rapids: Baker Academic, 2016), 290. Emphasis mine.

56. Duby, *Divine Simplicity*, 220.

proximity with each other in the "circulation of the divine life," but a mechanism by which to unite the divine persons as *one*. Where *perichoresis* may make oneness among the three persons possible, divine simplicity makes it necessary.[57]

These remarks should give us pause with regard to how we proceed in trinitarian theology. The recent trend has been to begin with a study of the trinitarian relations and persons and then to proceed to a consideration of the divine nature. But as Ortlund shows, without first grasping certain truths about the divine existence and essence—most importantly, divine simplicity—there is no guarantee that one's doctrine of the trinitarian relations and persons will be necessarily monotheistic. In fact, it is hard to see why one's account of God's threefold relations would be monotheistic if one were not already committed to the simplicity of the divine being.

Weaker Accounts of Compositional Unity

As noted above, many evangelical theistic mutualists are wary of embracing social trinitarianism. And they have good reasons to be. Nevertheless, it is hard to see how one can avoid drifting in the direction of social trinitarianism apart from adherence to the doctrine of simplicity. Thus, even among those conservative theistic mutualists who conscientiously steer clear of social trinitarianism, one detects distinct elements of the social model.

The more cautious accounts of compositional unity manifest their affinity with social trinitarianism in particular when it is argued that the three persons of the Godhead are three centers of consciousness with three distinct wills. Often this communal account of divine knowledge and will is found alongside traditional affirmation of the persons' identity of substance and essence. John Feinberg, for instance, states in classical fashion that the persons "must share the divine essence which is numerically one." He plainly affirms that the three

---

57. Gavin Ortlund, "Divine Simplicity in Historical Perspective: Resourcing a Contemporary Discussion," *International Journal of Systematic Theology* 16 (October 2014): 452.

distinct persons are "modes or subsistences of one essence" and even points out that "to deny this is to lapse either into tritheism on the one hand or modalism on the other."[58] Though Feinberg believes the persons share the same essence, he also attributes really distinct acts of knowledge and will to the persons individually. He makes this point as part of his argument that God is not always consciously thinking of all that He knows:

> Scripture depicts the members of the Godhead in conversation with one another.... But if God is always consciously aware of everything he knows, since all three members of the Trinity have this characteristic, how is fellowship within the Godhead possible? One member cannot draw the attention of another to one particular thing they know, because their attention is always fully on everything. Moreover, there is no reason to suspect that one member might be thinking of something that another is not thinking of, for all of them are always thinking of everything. So, if God is always consciously aware of everything he knows, then talk of fellowship within the Godhead must be anthropomorphic, and it is very difficult to know what such anthropomorphism means. On the other hand, if the members of the Godhead are not always thinking of everything they know, then conversation, drawing of attention to one particular truth they know, and fellowship are possible.[59]

While from the perspective of classical Christian theism numerous objections can be raised against this statement,[60] we should note particularly the challenge it poses to God's unity of substance. Thinking,

---

58. Feinberg, *No One Like Him*, 485.

59. Feinberg, *No One Like Him*, 318–19.

60. In addition to breaking up the substantial unity of God's mind and will, this passage effectively denies God's timeless eternity and endorses a doctrine of divine unconsciousness. It is but a small step from proposing that certain divine persons have peculiar acts of knowledge of which the other two divine persons are unaware to the proposition that God is also unaware of human thoughts and concerns. Once the scope of God's actual awareness and knowledge has been rendered finite, there is no reason this finiteness of divine consciousness should not also hold with respect to the concerns of creatures. In following out this line of reasoning, Feinberg suggests that our prayers actually move God to new acts of knowledge and thus make our fellowship with Him

knowing, and willing cannot on this account be properly aspects of God's essence (or substantial form) inasmuch as Feinberg isolates acts of knowledge to individual persons while denying them of the other two. Moreover, in order to remind the other divine persons of those bits of data of which they are allegedly unaware, the one who is in the act of knowing must intend to share it with the others. Thus the persons are possessed of discrete acts of will as well. The result of this is that divine knowing and willing are distinguished from the divine essence; and to the extent we say God knows or God wills, it can only be the result of discrete personal acts of knowing and willing coalescing together. The divine mind is hereby reduced to a form of "group thinking." This compositional unity of God's mind and volition appears to be an inchoate form of social trinitarianism.

Another way in which some recent Calvinist theologians advance the notion of a compositional unity of divine knowledge and will is through the teaching of eternal functional subordination. In short, this teaching claims that the Son is eternally subordinate to the Father such that the Father has a unique power and authority to issue commands to the Son, and the Son, in turn, has the unique obligation to submit Himself to the Father's command. Thus, each possesses a power of will that is really distinct from the other. What makes this claim controversial is that this command-obedience arrangement is said to characterize the relations of the persons within the Godhead itself (*ad intra*) and not merely to characterize the Son's obligation as incarnate man. Bruce Ware and Wayne Grudem are among the most well-known proponents of this view. Ware writes, "The Father possesses the place of supreme authority, and the Son is the eternal Son of the eternal Father. As such, the Son submits to the Father just as the Father, as the eternal Father of the eternal Son, exercises authority over the Son. And the Spirit submits to both the Father and the Son." He adds that "each Person is fully equal to each other in their commonly possessed essence."[61] As with

---

more understandable. "If God is not always thinking of everything he knows," Feinberg writes, "talk of fellowship with him makes more sense." *No One Like Him*, 319.

61. Bruce A. Ware, *Father, Son, and Holy Spirit: Relationships, Roles, and Relevance* (Wheaton, Ill.: Crossway, 2005), 21.

Feinberg's view, it would seem that the power of command and will are not properly aspects of the shared essence since these features are not common to the three persons. Wayne Grudem rejects the classical view that relations of origin (begetter, begotten, spirated) are sufficient to account for the real distinctions among the divine persons. Rather, he insists that real distinction among the persons is constituted by a structure of authority and submission that exists among them. He writes, "If we do not have economic subordination, then there is no inherent difference in the way the three persons relate to one another, and consequently we do not have the three distinct persons existing as Father, Son, and Holy Spirit for all eternity. For example, if the Son is not eternally subordinate to the Father in role, then the Father is not eternally 'Father' and the Son is not eternally 'Son.' This would mean that the Trinity has not eternally existed."[62]

For my present purposes, I shall pass over the many nuances of this current debate[63] and simply observe that if the Father should exercise a divine power and authority that is lacking in the Son, or if the Son should perform a divine volitional action (which would be necessarily involved in any act of submission) that the Father does not, then it would be difficult to see how the power of God and the will of God are anything other than the collective aggregation of individual faculties and acts of the persons. In other words, the singular power of God and will of God need not be one in any sense other than that of moral collaboration and agreement. More to the point, it would seem they

---

62. Grudem, *Systematic Theology*, 251. By "economic subordination," Grudem does not mean the *ad extra* work of the Son as incarnate in the economy of history but rather an economy of function that takes place within the Godhead itself. In this economy the Son submits as *divine* Son. Elsewhere he states that the "Father has *eternally* had a role of leadership, initiation, and primary authority among the members of the Trinity, and that the Son has *eternally* been subject to the Father's authority.'"Biblical Evidence for the Eternal Submission of the Son to the Father," in *The New Evangelical Subordinationism?*, 223.

63. For detailed arguments on both sides of this question, see Jowers and House, eds., *The New Evangelical Subordinationism?*. For a critique of the notion that humility and obedience characterize the divine persons in their *ad intra* relations, see Guy Mansini, "Can Humility and Obedience Be Trinitarian Realities?", in *Thomas Aquinas and Karl Barth: An Unofficial Catholic-Protestant Dialogue*, ed. Bruce L. McCormack and Thomas Joseph White (Grand Rapids: Eerdmans, 2013), 71–98.

cannot be one except through a corporate unity of purpose and agreement since eternal functional subordination requires that the volition of the Father, Son, and Spirit be three really distinct volitional acts.[64] This appears to be a step in the direction of social trinitarianism. On this teaching, substantial unity no longer accounts for the unity of power, intellect, or will in the Godhead.

Conclusion

It is not my contention that the various compositional accounts considered above necessarily represent instances of tritheism. Indeed, the monotheistic commitment of most of the theologians who advance compositional versions of divine unity is beyond question. The challenge lies in explaining precisely why a tritheistic reconception of the data would be absolutely impossible. And this is the concern. If the one God exists in three really distinct persons, how do we know that God's unity is not a social unity of three distinct divine beings or a compound unity of three parts who are each less than fully divine and upon which divinity itself depends? Either of these approaches would still allow one to confess that God is one without requiring commitment to monotheism per se. What is needed is an understanding of divine unity that *necessarily* proscribes every possible trithesitic construal of the biblical data. And only a unity of simplicity provides that. It is perhaps inevitable that without conscientious adherence to the doctrine of simplicity there will be at least some measure of fraying around the edges of the fabric of monotheism. This is the trinitarian dilemma facing theistic mutualists.

---

64. It is surely no coincidence that those evangelicals who argue for the Son's eternal functional subordination to the Father generally do so in the context of discussing the importance of corporate unity among creatures. The Trinity is deployed as a blueprint for human communal union and agreeableness. For instance, Ware commends authority-submission roles in certain human relations as a way of following the trinitarian pattern. "The most marked characteristic of the trinitarian relationships," he writes, "is the presence of an eternal and inherent expression of authority and submission. *Both authority and submission are good, for both are expressive of God himself.*" *Father, Son, and Holy Spirit,* 137. For an evenhanded response from the classical perspective, see Fred Sanders, "The Trinity in Gender Debates," *The Scriptorium Daily,* October 30, 2012, http://www.patheos.com/blogs/scriptorium/2012/10/the-Trinity-in-gender-debates/.

CHAPTER 7

Conclusion

It is difficult to overstate the contrast between the older outlook of classical Christian theism and the newer viewpoint of theistic mutualism. These two approaches to the doctrine of God are not two slightly different ways of saying basically the same thing. The classical view insists upon God's unchanging plentitude of being, while the mutualist view believes such an emphasis presents a barrier to the possibility of creatures enjoying a significant relationship with God. For God to be personally related to His creatures in a significant way, we are told, He must be involved in reciprocity and change—in short, a mutualistic relation with us in which He both gives and receives. The mutualist view is of a God who becomes in some respect what He previously was not.

Nevertheless, many evangelical theistic mutualists are wary of abandoning the claims of classical theism altogether. They desire to continue confessing that God is self-sufficient, infinite, eternal, and unchanging. In order to accommodate the demands of both the classical and mutualist approaches, they propose that God is all that classical theism claims with respect to His essence, while He is all that theistic mutualism requires with respect to those aspects of His being that are not part of His essence. But as I have argued in various places throughout this volume, from the classical perspective this both/and approach to theism is impossible due to the fact that it violates the fundamental grammar of divine simplicity. And without simplicity, it is not clear that any of the other claims classical theists tend to make about God can be true. Without simplicity, God must be dependent on something other than His divinity for some aspects of His being, and thus He cannot be *a se* and independent. Without simplicity, God is open to the acquisition of being in addition to His essence and thus is not immutable. Without simplicity, it is not clear why God could not experience temporal change and thus fail to be timelessly eternal. Without simplicity, it is impossible that God be in every way infinite as there must be parts in Him, and parts by definition must be finite. Moreover, that which is built of parts cannot be infinite since the finite cannot aggregately yield the infinite. Many more such arguments could be arranged. But it should be clear that one cannot shrug off or lessen the demands of divine simplicity and imagine that the edifice of classical theism will remain fairly well intact. Yet this seems to be precisely what many evangelical theistic mutualists have mistakenly assumed.

We must conclude that theistic mutualism is not a promising way forward. It consistently undermines numerous features of the biblically and classically orthodox Christian doctrine of God, most especially those features vital to upholding God's absoluteness of being. Furthermore, it is plainly wrong about the alleged liabilities of the classical approach. The traditional doctrines do not need to be replaced or supplemented by more dynamic and lively notions of God. In fact, the God of classical Christian theism is infinitely more concerned with the welfare and conduct of His creatures than the God of theistic mutualism could ever be. This is because on the classical account God's concern and care do not come and go; they do not rise and fall. They are one and the same as His eternal act of creation and, for His elect, the same as His eternal decree to do them good through the salvation He provides in His Son. These virtues by which God cares and provides for His creatures are purely and unchangingly actual in Him. They are not stirred up or actualized by the actions of His creatures upon Him. God cannot be made more compassionate toward sinners or more opposed to sin than He is from all eternity. This is because it is His nature to love, and it is His nature to detest sin. These are not mere potentialities in His nature but rather are purely actual in Him inasmuch as they are identical with His act of being.

Moreover, God need not experience changes of relation in order to meaningfully relate Himself to His creatures. He need only ordain a change in the revelation of His unchanging being in accordance with

His wisdom and the needs and requirements of the creature in time. In this way, it is not God who changes but rather the manifestations of God, which are perfectly suited to the needs and circumstances of His creatures—whether according to wrath or according to mercy—at any given moment of their lives. It seems audacious to conclude that this unique manner of God's care for His creatures is somehow impersonal and lacking vibrancy. Why must God be personal and related to others in the same way as finite persons are? Why must He undergo change in order for His love or opposition to sin to be regarded as genuine? Indeed, it would seem that the One who is unchanging, simple, and purely actual in all that He is—which is exactly what classical theism claims about God—is the One who is most profoundly vibrant and powerful in relating Himself to others. Such a God may appear strange and unlike us in many significant respects. Nevertheless, one thing is clear: classical theism is not in need of a replacement model, as all other models must fall short of the true confession of God's infinite fullness of being—the confession that all that is in God is God.

Bibliography

À Brakel, Wilhelmus. *The Christian's Reasonable Service.* Edited by Joel R. Beeke. Translated by Bartel Elshout. 4 volumes. Grand Rapids: Reformation Heritage Books, 1992.

Ames, William. *The Marrow of Theology.* Translated by John Dykstra Eusden. Boston: Pilgrim Press, 1968.

Anderson, James. *The Cause of Being: The Philosophy of Creation in St. Thomas.* St. Louis: B. Herder, 1952.

Anselm. *Proslogion.* In *Anselm: Basic Writings.* Translated and edited by Thomas Williams. Indianapolis: Hackett, 2007.

Athanasius. *Against the Heathen.* Volume 4 of *The Nicene and Post-Nicene Fathers.* Edited by Phillip Schaff and Henry Wace. Grand Rapids: Eerdmans, 1953.

———. De Decretis *or Defence of the Nicene Definition.* Volume 4 of *The Nicene and Post-Nicene Fathers.* Edited by Phillip Schaff and Henry Wace. Grand Rapids: Eerdmans, 1953.

———. *Four Discourses against the Arians.* Volume 4 of *The Nicene and Post-Nicene Fathers.* Edited by Phillip Schaff and Henry Wace. Grand Rapids: Eerdmans, 1953.

Augustine. *The City of God.* Translated by Marcus Dods. New York: Random House, 1950.

———. *The Confessions.* Edited by John E. Rotelle. Translated by Maria Boulding. Hyde Park, N.Y.: New City Press, 1997.

———. *The Trinity*. Edited by John E. Rotelle. Translated by Edmund Hill. Hyde Park, N.Y.: New City Press, 1991.

Ayres, Lewis. *Augustine and the Trinity*. Cambridge: Cambridge University Press, 2010.

———. *Nicaea and Its Legacy: An Approach to Fourth-Century Trinitarian Theology*. Oxford: Oxford University Press, 2004.

Baines, Ronald S., and Richard C. Barcellos, James P. Butler, Stefan T. Lindblad, James M. Renihan, eds. *Confessing the Impassible God: The Biblical, Classical, and Confessional Doctrine of Divine Impassibility*. Palmdale, Calif.: RBAP, 2015.

Barth, Karl. *Church Dogmatics*. Volume II/1, *The Doctrine of God*. Translated by T. H. L. Parker et al. Edinburgh: T&T Clark, 1957.

Bavinck, Herman. *Reformed Dogmatics*. Edited by John Bolt. Translated by John Vriend. 4 volumes. Grand Rapids: Baker Academic, 2004.

Berkhof, Louis. *Manual of Christian Doctrine*. Grand Rapids: Eerdmans, 1933.

———. *Systematic Theology*. Grand Rapids: Eerdmans, 1996.

Boethius. *Philosophiae Consolationis*. In *The Theological Tractates/The Consolation of Philosophy*. Translated by H. F. Stewart, E. K. Rand, and S. J. Tester. Cambridge, Mass.: Harvard University Press, 1973.

———. *De Trinitate*. In *The Theological Tractates/The Consolation of Philosophy*. Translated by H. F. Stewart, E. K. Rand, and S. J. Tester. Cambridge, Mass.: Harvard University Press, 1973.

Boyer, Steven D., and Christopher A. Hall. *The Mystery of God: A Theology for Knowing the Unknowable*. Grand Rapids: Baker Academic, 2012.

Buswell, J. Oliver. *A Systematic Theology of the Christian Religion*. 2 volumes in 1. Grand Rapids: Zondervan, 1962.

Calvin, John. *Sermons of Master John Calvin upon the Book of Job.* Translated by Arthur Golding. London: Impensis Georgij Bishop, 1574. Reprint, Edinburgh: Banner of Truth Trust, 1993.

Carson, D. A. *The Difficult Doctrine of the Love of God.* Wheaton, Ill.: Crossway, 2000.

Charnock, Stephen. *The Existence and Attributes of God.* 2 volumes. 1853. Reprint, Grand Rapids: Baker, 1979.

Cooper, Burton Z. *The Idea of God: A Whiteheadian Critique of St. Thomas Aquinas' Concept of God.* The Hague: Martinus Nijhoff, 1974.

Craig, William Lane. "Timelessness and Omnitemporality." In *God and Time: Four Views,* edited by Gregory E. Ganssle, 129–60. Downers Grove, Ill.: IVP Academic, 2001.

Dabney, R. L. *Discussions.* Vol. 1, *Theological and Evangelical.* 1890. Reprint, Harrisonburg, Va.: Sprinkle Publications, 1982.

Davies, Brian. *An Introduction to the Philosophy of Religion.* 3rd ed. Oxford: Oxford University Press, 2004.

———. "A Modern Defense of Divine Simplicity." In *Philosophy of Religion: A Guide and Anthology,* edited by Brian Davies, 549–64. Oxford: Oxford University Press, 2000.

Dennison, James T., Jr. *Reformed Confessions of the 16th and 17th Centuries in English Translation.* 4 volumes. Grand Rapids: Reformation Heritage Books, 2008–2014.

Denzinger, Henry, ed. *The Sources of Catholic Dogma.* Translated by Roy J. Deferrari. Fritzwilliam, N.H.: Loreto Publications, 2002.

De Raeymaeker, Louis. *The Philosophy of Being.* Translated by Edmund H. Ziegelmeyer. St. Louis: B. Herder, 1954.

Dodds, Michael J. *The Unchanging God of Love: Thomas Aquinas and Contemporary Theology on Divine Immutability.* 2nd ed.

Washington, D.C.: Catholic University of America Press, 2008.

Dolezal, James E. *God without Parts: Divine Simplicity and the Metaphysics of God's Absoluteness*. Eugene, Ore.: Pickwick Publications, 2011.

———. Review of *God Is Impassible and Impassioned: Toward a Theology of Divine Emotion*, by Rob Lister. *Westminster Theological Journal* 76 (Fall 2014): 414–18.

———. "Still Impassible: Confessing God without Passions." *Journal of the Institute of Reformed Baptist Studies* 1 (2014): 125–51.

———. "Trinity, Simplicity and the Status of God's Personal Relations." *International Journal of Systematic Theology* 16 (January 2014): 79–98.

Dorner, Isaak August. *Divine Immutability: A Critical Reconsideration*. Translated by Robert R. Williams and Claude Welch. Minneapolis: Fortress Press, 1994.

Duby, Steven J. *Divine Simplicity: A Dogmatic Account*. London: Bloomsbury T&T Clark, 2016.

Emery, Gilles. "The Immutability of the God of Love and the Problem of Language Concerning the 'Suffering of God.'" In *Divine Impassibility and the Mystery of Human Suffering*, edited by James F. Keating and Thomas Joseph White, 27–76. Grand Rapids: Eerdmans, 2009.

———. *The Trinitarian Theology of Saint Thomas Aquinas*. Translated by Francesca Aran Murphy. Oxford: Oxford University Press, 2007.

———. *The Trinity: An Introduction to the Catholic Doctrine of God*. Translated by Matthew Levering. Washington, D.C.: Catholic University of America Press, 2011.

———. *Trinity in Aquinas*. Ypsilanti, Mich.: Sapientia Press, 2003.

Erickson, Millard J. *God the Father Almighty: A Contemporary Exploration of the Divine Attributes.* Grand Rapids: Baker, 1998.

Feinberg, John S. *No One Like Him: The Doctrine of God.* Wheaton, Ill.: Crossway, 2001.

Frame, John M. *The Doctrine of God.* Phillipsburg, N.J.: P&R, 2002.

Garrigou-Lagrange, Réginald. *God: His Existence and His Nature.* Translated by Dom Bede Rose. 2 volumes. St. Louis: B. Herder, 1934.

Gaukroger, Stephen. *The Emergence of a Scientific Culture: Science and the Shaping of Modernity, 1210–1695.* Oxford: Clarendon, 2006.

Gill, John. *A Body of Divinity.* Grand Rapids: Sovereign Grace Publishers, 1971.

Gilson, Etienne. *Being and Some Philosophers.* 2nd ed. Toronto: Pontifical Institute of Mediaeval Studies, 1952.

———. *The Christian Philosophy of St. Thomas Aquinas.* Translated by L. K. Shook. New York: Random House, 1956.

Goris, Harm. "Thomism in Zanchi's Doctrine of God." In *Reformation and Scholasticism: An Ecumenical Enterprise,* edited by Willem J. van Asselt and Eef Dekker, 121–39. Grand Rapids: Baker Academic, 2001.

Gregory of Nyssa. *Against Eunomius.* In volume 5 of *A Select Library of Nicene and Post-Nicene Fathers of the Christian Church: Second Series.* Edited by Philip Schaff and Henry Mace. Translated by William Moore and Henry Austin Wilson. Grand Rapids: Eerdmans, 1979.

———. *On the Holy Spirit.* In volume 5 of *A Select Library of Nicene and Post-Nicene Fathers of the Christian Church: Second Series.* Edited by Philip Schaff and Henry Mace. Translated by William Moore and Henry Austin Wilson. Grand Rapids: Eerdmans, 1979.

Grudem, Wayne. "Biblical Evidence for the Eternal Submission of the Son to the Father." In *The New Evangelical Subordinationism? Perspectives on the Equality of God the Father and God the Son*, edited by Dennis W. Jowers and H. Wayne House, 223–61. Eugene, Ore.: Pickwick Publications, 2012.

———. *Systematic Theology: An Introduction to Biblical Doctrine.* Grand Rapids: Zondervan, 1994.

Hart, David Bentley. *The Experience of God: Being, Consciousness, Bliss.* New Haven, Conn.: Yale University Press, 2013.

Hartshorne, Charles. *The Divine Relativity: A Social Conception of God.* New Haven, Conn.: Yale University Press, 1948.

Helm, Paul. "Eternal Creation." *Tyndale Bulletin* 45 (1994): 321–38.

———. *Eternal God: A Study of God without Time.* 2nd ed. Oxford: Oxford University Press, 2010.

———. "Response by Paul Helm." In *Perspectives on the Doctrine of God: Four Views*, edited by Bruce A. Ware, 121–29. Nashville: B&H Academic, 2008.

Hodge, A. A. *The Confession of Faith.* 1869. Reprint, London: Banner of Truth Trust, 1958.

———. *Outlines of Theology.* 1879. Reprint, Edinburgh: Banner of Truth Trust, 1972.

Hodge, Charles. *Systematic Theology.* 3 volumes. Grand Rapids: Eerdmans, 1952.

Holmes, Stephen R. *The Quest for the Trinity: The Doctrine of God in Scripture, History and Modernity.* Downers Grove, Ill.: IVP Academic, 2012.

———. "Something Much Too Plain to Say: Towards a Defense of the Doctrine of Divine Simplicity." *Neue Zeitschrift für Systematische Theologie und Religionsphilosophie* 43 (2001): 137–54.

———. "Three Versus One? Some Problems of Social Trinitarianism." *Journal of Reformed Theology* 3 (2009): 77–89.

Irenaeus. *Against Heresies*. In *The Apostolic Fathers—Justine Martyr—Irenaeus*. Volume 1 of *The Ante-Nicene Fathers*. Edited by Alexander Roberts and James Donaldson. Translated by Ernest Cushing Richardson and Bernhard Pick. New York: Charles Scribner's Sons, 1903.

John of Damascus. *On Heresies*. In *Saint John of Damascus: Writings*. Translated by Frederic H. Chase Jr. The Fathers of the Church. Volume 37. New York: Fathers of the Church, Inc., 1958.

Journet, Charles. *The Meaning of Evil*. Translated by Michael Barry. New York: P. J. Kennedy and Sons, 1963.

Jowers, Dennis W. "The Inconceivability of Subordination within a Simple God." In *The New Evangelical Subordinationism? Perspectives on the Equality of God the Father and God the Son*, edited by Dennis W. Jowers and H. Wayne House, 375–410. Eugene, Ore.: Pickwick Publications, 2012.

Joyce, George Hayward. *Principles of Natural Theology*. 3rd ed. London: Longmans, Green, 1951.

Leigh, Edward. *A Systeme or Body of Divinity*. London: William Lee, 1662.

Levering, Matthew. *Engaging the Doctrine of the Holy Spirit: Love and Gift in the Trinity and the Church*. Grand Rapids: Baker Academic, 2016.

———. *Scripture and Metaphysics: Aquinas and the Renewal of Trinitarian Theology*. Oxford: Blackwell Publishing, 2004.

Lister, Rob. *God Is Impassible and Impassioned: Toward a Theology of Divine Emotion*. Wheaton, Ill.: Crossway, 2012.

Macleod, Donald. *Shared Life: The Trinity and the Fellowship of God's People*. Fearn, Ross-shire: Christian Focus, 1994.

Mansini, Guy. "Can Humility and Obedience Be Trinitarian Realities?" In *Thomas Aquinas and Karl Barth: An Unofficial Catholic-*

Protestant Dialogue, edited by Bruce L. McCormack and Thomas Joseph White, 71–98. Grand Rapids: Eerdmans, 2013.

Mascall, E. L. *He Who Is: A Study in Traditional Theism.* London: Longmans, Green, 1943.

McCabe, Herbert. *God Matters.* London: Geoffrey Chapman, 1987.

Moltmann, Jürgen. *The Trinity and the Kingdom: The Doctrine of God.* Translated by Margaret Kohl. San Francisco: Harper & Row, 1981.

Moreland, J. P., and William Lane Craig. *Philosophical Foundations for a Christian Worldview.* Downers Grove, Ill.: IVP Academic, 2003.

Muller, Richard A. "The Dogmatic Function of St. Thomas' 'Proofs': A Protestant Appreciation." *Fides et Historia* 24 (1992): 15–29.

———. "Incarnation, Immutability, and the Case for Classical Theism." *Westminster Theological Journal* 45 (Spring 1983): 22–40.

———. *Post-Reformation Reformed Dogmatics: The Rise and Development of Reformed Orthodoxy, ca. 1520–1725.* 4 volumes. Grand Rapids: Baker Academic, 2003.

Mullins, R. T. *The End of the Timeless God.* Oxford: Oxford University Press, 2016.

Nash, Ronald H. *The Concept of God: An Exploration of Contemporary Difficulties with the Attributes of God.* Grand Rapids: Zondervan, 1983.

Nichols, Aidan. *Discovering Aquinas: An Introduction to His Life, Work, and Influence.* Grand Rapids: Eerdmans, 2003.

Oliphint, K. Scott. *God with Us: Divine Condescension and the Attributes of God.* Wheaton, Ill.: Crossway, 2012.

Ortlund, Gavin. "Divine Simplicity in Historical Perspective: Resourcing a Contemporary Discussion." *International Journal of Systematic Theology* 16 (October 2014): 436–53.

Owen, John. *A Brief Vindication and Declaration of the Doctrine of the Trinity*. Volume 2 of *The Works of John Owen*. Edited by William Goold. 1850–1853. Reprint, Edinburgh: Banner of Truth Trust, 1997.

———. *The Glory of Christ*. Volume 1 of *The Works of John Owen*. Edited by William Goold. 1850–1853. Reprint, Edinburgh: Banner of Truth Trust, 1999.

———. *A Practical Exposition upon Psalm CXXX*. Volume 6 of *The Works of John Owen*. Edited by William Goold. 1850–1853. Reprint, Edinburgh: Banner of Truth Trust, 2000.

———. *Vindicae Evangelicae*. Volume 12 of *The Works of John Owen*. Edited by William Goold. 1850–1853. Reprint, Edinburgh: Banner of Truth Trust, 1999.

Owens, Joseph. *An Interpretation of Existence*. Milwaukee, Wis.: Bruce, 1968.

Packer, J. I. *Concise Theology: A Guide to Historic Christian Beliefs*. Carol Stream, Ill.: Tyndale House, 1993.

———. "Theism for Our Time." In *God Who Is Rich in Mercy*, edited by Peter T. O'Brien and David G. Peterson, 1–23. Grand Rapids: Baker, 1986.

Perkins, William. *A Golden Chaine: or, The Description of Theology*. In *The Workes of That Famous and Worthy Minister of Christ in the Universitie of Cambridge, Mr. William Perkins*. 3 volumes. London: John Legatt, 1626.

Pink, Arthur W. *Gleanings in the Godhead*. Chicago: Moody, 1975.

Pinnock, Clark H. *Most Moved Mover: A Theology of God's Openness*. Grand Rapids: Baker Academic, 2001.

Pinnock, Clark, Richard Rice, John Sanders, William Hasker, and David Basinger. *The Openness of God: A Biblical Challenge to the Traditional Understanding of God*. Downers Grove, Ill: IVP, 1994.

Plantinga, Alvin. *Does God Have a Nature?* Milwaukee, Wis.: Marquette University Press, 1980.

Plantinga, Cornelius, Jr. "Social Trinity and Tritheism." In *A Reader in Contemporary Philosophical Theology*, edited by Oliver D. Crisp, 67–89. London: T&T Clark, 2009.

Prestige, G. L. *God in Patristic Thought*. London: S.P.C.K., 1952.

Radde-Gallwitz, Andrew. *Basil of Caesarea, Gregory of Nyssa, and the Transformation of Divine Simplicity*. Oxford: Oxford University Press, 2009.

Renihan, Samuel, ed. *God without Passions: A Reader*. Palmdale, Calif.: RBAP, 2015.

Reymond, Robert L. *A New Systematic Theology of the Christian Faith*. Nashville: Thomas Nelson, 1998.

Rocca, Gregory P. *Speaking the Incomprehensible God: Thomas Aquinas on the Interplay of Positive and Negative Theology*. Washington, D.C.: Catholic University of America Press, 2004.

Runggaldier, Edmund. "Divine Eternity as Timeless Perfection." *European Journal for Philosophy of Religion* 8 (Summer 2016): 169–82.

Sanlon, Peter. *Simply God: Recovering the Classical Trinity*. Nottingham, England: Inter-Varsity, 2014.

Shanley, Brian J. *The Thomist Tradition*. Dordrecht: Springer, 2002.

Sheed, F. J. "The Modern Attitude to God." In *God: Papers Read at the Summer School of Catholic Studies, Held at Cambridge, July 26th—August 4th, 1930*, edited by C. Lattey, 217–34. London: Sheed and Ward, 1931.

Smith, Timothy. *Thomas Aquinas' Trinitarian Theology: A Study in Theological Method*. Washington, D.C.: Catholic University of America Press, 2003.

Swain, Scott R. "Divine Trinity." In *Christian Dogmatics: Reformed Theology for the Church Catholic*, edited by Michael Allen and

Scott R. Swain, 78–106. Grand Rapids: Baker Academic, 2016.

Swinnock, George. *The Incomparableness of God*. Volume 4 of *The Works of George Swinnock*. 1868. Reprint, Edinburgh: Banner of Truth Trust, 1992.

Te Velde, Rudi A. *Aquinas on God: The 'Divine Science' of the* Summa Theologiae. Aldershot, U.K.: Ashgate, 2006.

Thomas Aquinas. *Compendium theologiae*. Translated by Cyril Vollert as *Compendium of Theology*. St. Louis: B. Herder, 1947.

———. *Scriptum super libros Sententiarum*. Translated by E. M. Macierowski as *Thomas Aquinas's Earliest Treatment of the Divine Essence:* Scriptum super libros Sententiarum, *Book I, Distinction 8*. Binghamton, N.Y.: Binghamton University, 1998.

———. *Summa contra Gentiles*. Translated by Anton C. Pegis, James F. Anderson, Vernon J. Bourke and Charles J. O'Neil as *On the Truth of the Catholic Faith*. 5 volumes. Garden City, N.Y.: Doubleday, 1955.

———. *Summa theologiae*. Translated by Fathers of the English Dominican Province as *Summa Theologica*. 5 volumes. Allen, Tex.: Christian Classics, 1981.

Thornwell, James Henley. *The Collected Writings of James Henley Thornwell*. 4 volumes. Edinburgh: Banner of Truth Trust, 1986.

Torrance, Thomas F. *The Christian Doctrine of God, One Being Three Persons*. Edinburgh: T&T Clark, 1996.

Tracy, Thomas F. *God, Action, and Embodiment*. Grand Rapids: Eerdmans, 1984.

Turretin, Francis. *Institutes of Elenctic Theology*. Edited by James T. Dennison Jr. Translated by George Musgrave Giger. 3 volumes. Phillipsburg, N.J.: P&R, 1992–1997.

Twisse, William. *A Discovery of D. Jacksons Vanitie*. London: N.p., 1631.

Van den Brink, Gijsbert. "Social Trinitarianism: A Discussion of Some Recent Theological Criticisms." *International Journal of Systematic Theology* 16 (July 2014): 331–50.

Vanhoozer, Kevin J. *Remythologizing Theology: Divine Action, Passion, and Authorship.* Cambridge: Cambridge University Press, 2010.

Vos, Geerhardus. *Theology Proper.* Vol. 1 of *Reformed Dogmatics.* Translated and edited by Richard B. Gaffin Jr. Bellingham, Wash.: Lexham Press, 2014.

Ware, Bruce A. "Defining Evangelicalism's Boundaries Theologically: Is Open Theism Evangelical?" *Journal of the Evangelical Theological Society* 45 (June 2002): 193–212.

———. "An Evangelical Reformulation of the Doctrine of the Immutability of God." *Journal of the Evangelical Theological Society* 29 (December 1986): 431–46.

———. "An Exposition and Critique of the Process Doctrines of Divine Mutability and Immutability." *Westminster Theological Journal* 47 (1985): 175–96.

———. *Father, Son, and Holy Spirit: Relationships, Roles, and Relevance.* Wheaton, Ill.: Crossway, 2005.

———. *God's Greater Glory: The Exalted God of Scripture and the Christian Faith.* Wheaton, Ill.: Crossway, 2004.

———. *God's Lesser Glory: The Diminished God of Open Theism.* Wheaton, Ill.: Crossway, 2000.

———. "A Modified Calvinist Doctrine of God." In *Perspectives on the Doctrine of God: Four Views,* edited by Bruce A. Ware, 76–120. Nashville: B&H Academic, 2008.

Watson, Thomas. *A Body of Divinity.* London: Banner of Truth Trust, 1958.

Webster, John. "Life in and of Himself: Reflections on God's Aseity." In *Engaging the Doctrine of God: Contemporary Protestant*

Perspectives, edited by Bruce L. McCormack, 107–24. Grand Rapids: Baker Academic, 2008.

Weigel, Peter. *Aquinas on Simplicity: An Investigation into the Foundations of His Philosophical Theology*. Oxford: Peter Lang, 2008.

Weinandy, Thomas G. *Does God Suffer?* Notre Dame, Ind.: University of Notre Dame Press, 2000.

White, Thomas Joseph. "Divine Simplicity and the Holy Trinity." *International Journal of Systematic Theology* 18 (January 2016): 66–93.

———. "Nicene Orthodoxy and Trinitarian Simplicity." *American Catholic Philosophical Quarterly* 90 (Fall 2016): 727–50.

Wippel, John F. *The Metaphysical Thought of Thomas Aquinas: From Finite Being to Uncreated Being*. Washington, D.C.: Catholic University of America Press, 2000.

Wolterstorff, Nicholas. "God Everlasting." In *Philosophy of Religion: A Guide and Anthology*, edited by Brian Davies, 485–504. Oxford: Oxford University Press, 2000.

Young, Frances M. *From Nicaea to Chalcedon: A Guide to the Literature and Its Background*. 2nd ed. Grand Rapids: Baker Academic, 2010.

Zanchius, Girolamo. *Life Everlasting*. Edited by Robert Hill. Cambridge: John Legat, 1601.

Scripture Index

Subject Index